# THE 5 YEAR JOURNAL™

### DOREENE CLEMENT

# THE 5 YEAR JOURNAL

By DOREENE CLEMENT

INTERNET: http://www.The5YearJournal.com

For information regarding purchasing THE 5 YEAR JOURNAL

Published by:
Triangulus 3 Marketing
5025 N Central Avenue
Suite 444
Phoenix, AZ 85012

ISBN: 978-0-578-14760-4

Printed by: Outskirts Press

PRINTED IN THE UNITED STATES OF AMERICA

# This Journal Belongs To
*if found please return to*

Name: _____

Address: _____

City: _____ State: _____ Zip: _____

Country: _____

Phone: _____

Email Address: _____


Day I Started This Journal: _____
*(This Journal can be started on any day of any year.)*


Day I Completed This Journal: _____

# THE 5 YEAR JOURNAL

By DOREENE CLEMENT

I would like to thank everyone who has been involved with me and THE 5 YEAR JOURNAL for their endless love and support; all those who have purchased 5YJ; all those who have used 5YJ; and all those who have believed not only in me, but the endless value of 5YJ.

Love to You All!
Doreene Clement

I would like to give gratitude and appreciation to Doreene Clement for her friendship, faith and trust in me to carry on the legacy of The 5 Year Journal. As it was my sacred honor to help care for Doreene during her health challenges from early 2004 to June 14, 2007, the date of her passing; it is my privilege and my joy to keep her vision and dream for The 5 Year Journal alive.

A very special thank you to all my family, friends, coaches, advisors, and colleagues. With an extra special gratitude to one of Doreene's biggest fans and dearest friend, Rita Davenport. Her love, support and friendship for Doreene was precious and sacred. And, her encouragement to me to continue making The 5YJ available is special beyond words or measure. And, most importantly, a heartfelt gratitude to the ten's of thousands of users of The 5 Year Journal who have encouraged me to embrace this honor and keep the dream and the legacy of The 5 Year Journal alive on Doreene's behalf.

In Loving Appreciation & Gratitude!
Sandy Rogers

# THE 5 YEAR JOURNAL

## Table of Contents

# THE 5 YEAR JOURNAL

## Introduction — The Purpose

Where were you a year ago?

What were you doing 2 years ago?

What were you feeling 3 years ago?

What were your dreams 4 years ago?

What were your accomplishments 5 years ago?

**THE 5 YEAR JOURNAL** is a timely tool for The New Millennium. It will enable you to journalize and plan the next 5 years with what you want, what you have felt, and where you have been. Year by year your entries add to the total summary of your feelings and events, until, on one page you can look back at the past years, up to 5 years – day by day – thought by thought – experience by experience.

We tend to be hard on ourselves, not always giving ourselves the credit due for what growth and change has occurred. Journalizing in this Journal and in the Workbook sections, over a 5 year period will memorialize what was happening. Then having 5 years to look back upon, at one glance, can give us a more accurate reflection of what did or did not happen in the past.

Recording a relative reflection creates an accurate record of memories that we can then use for assessment and personal growth. This Journal will be a reminder and support, or where we have been and where we want to go with our lives. Even if you already journal, THE 5 YEAR JOURNAL can be effective in addition to what you are currently doing. This Journal can be a quick and easy tool for highlights and learning from hindsight. THE 5 YEAR JOURNAL has a unique design that allows you to start journaling any day of the year.

With the passage of time we gain a different perspective. Time is a healer and what was once hard or unbearable can now make more sense, giving us a clearer picture. Recording and tracking our lives in this Journal can actually bring relief, clarity, joy and laughter. You can also use the Month End Summary, Quarterly Questions, Year End Favorites, The Best and Worst Things That Happened to Me, Q and A Year End, Create Your Own Topic, and Year End Summary as meters to track experiences at a glance.

Imagine sitting down, just you or with friends, remembering that favorite movie or favorite song, reading about what you were doing, what you were feeling, or what was happening in your life on a specific date. With this Journal there will be a first-hand account of what was, what had happened to you in your life. With the distance and time in-between, you may have a new experience with your past and create a more rewarding future. Imagine passing this Journal on to a friend or family member so they could know you and your history. They could feel your joys and successes, and experience your pains and sorrows.

This Journal can also be used for personal or business items, recording important dates, future deadlines, anniversaries, and more. Dates important in the future can now be pre-recorded for a manner of easy reminding.

The most important idea to remember about THE 5 YEAR JOURNAL is that you now have a quick and easy-to-use tool that can be an asset for your well-being. It can enhance and assist you in the many ways that you choose to use it. It can be fun.     ~     Doreene Clement

# THE 5 YEAR JOURNAL

## Doreene Clement's Reflections

**You can Journal daily in just minutes in THE 5 YEAR JOURNAL.**

**Easily summarize your day, create a gratitude journal, a health or diet journal, a prayer or dream journal, track your goals and intentions and so much more, within these pages. If you want to journal more, use a blank book first then come back to 5YJ.**

## For me, Journalizing is Remembering.

To accurately and honestly remember the subtle details of personal and emotional experiences, I like to write them down. Writing makes what I want to express more solid. It allows me to be more aware and conscious. It helps me to not only visualize, but I feel a sense of release and relief after writing.

I sometimes discount my accomplishments, not always giving to myself, the support and recognition of what I've actually achieved and to what degree. Through the years friends have supported and reminded me of my successes and accomplishments, but my particular personal slant sometimes discounts my own growth, gain, and success. This is one reason I started to write, to Journal my life.

Through Journals I learned that I am usually doing better than the credit I give to myself. I can easily stop myself from going into a negative binge. I use my Journal to remember, the tool and the advantage that hindsight can be.

Another reason I started to write in Journals was because there is something that happens after I write about my thoughts, feelings, and experiences more easily. Writing helps to free my mind – and focus. I am more creative and can create and hold new thoughts more easily, because I have made the room in my mind and with my time. Writing helps me to heal.

I have learned not to live in my past experiences. I now reflect back for lessons rather than dwell in the past. I can now use the past as a resource. I have even problem solved and invented in my dreams, waking in the middle of the night to record my dreams and ideas.

On the days that I make a list of "things to do," it organizes what I want to accomplish for the day – and it organizes me. It organizes my thoughts and focuses my direction. The things I have to do may change. I can leave something off the list, or not get to some of the items, but it is all written down. Nothing gets lost. There is a focus and my tasks are made solid. As I finish each task I cross it off my list, gaining the feeling that I have accomplished my goals. I have created a success, some large and some small, but successes all.

Journalizing does the same for my thoughts and emotions. I make a list of where I've been, what I'm feeling, and what I'm doing. I itemize through the writing – where I am, what my fears are, what I'm happy about. I create a current and ongoing truthful inventory of me.

My Journalizing helps me remember to remember. I can change my mind. I can feel differently. I can make mistakes. Right then and there – when it was written down – that was where I was at that moment. Through the years I have come to know myself better. I have come to accept more of myself. I have learned and am learning still. I have gained and I can say I have changed and can change some more. I know these facts about myself because I kept a record. A written record.

Through the years I've received and bought beautiful Journals – some were even leather bound with wonderful papers. Yet, some of my thoughts would end up on scraps of paper. I like ease and convenience so I decided to organize my writing – and create a method to write in – so I designed THE 5 YEAR JOURNAL.

With Love,

Doreene Clement

# Sample Page from Doreene's Original Personal Journal

## The Best Thing That Happened To Me This Year Was...

1945 - Moved in & Remodeled my house - turned it into my home. Added places & Features that made it me.

1996 - Mom moved back to Phoenix from Las Vegas - its nice to have her home.

1997 - Spent alot of time in mexico. It's a very Healthy place for me to be. love the vibe.

1998 - Wrote more than ever this year - and that's wonderful.

1999 - Published · The 5 year Journal YEAH !!!

# THE 5 YEAR JOURNAL

## How To Use This Journal

**Use your Journal to capture and summarize your daily experiences thoughts, and feelings.**

A good place to start as you begin to think about **your** Journal – is to simply remember to breathe. In other words – be light. Let yourself relax into the thoughts and ideas you have, let them flow. **Remember...this is your Journal.** What goes inside these pages is totally up to you and no one else.

- You can start using your Journal any day of the year.

- Each Journal page covers two calendar days for 5 years, allowing a reference and comparative look at the same dates for 5 years.

- The beauty of this Journal is having on one page, in one Journal, in one place, a comparative of your times and your experiences giving you a clearer picture of your past.

- Ease into the routine of daily writing so you can get into the habit of writing in our Journal every day.

- Keep your Journal within your daily routine. Set it where you will see it, someplace you'll look every day, a place where it will trigger your memory daily – so it is easy to write down a thought, a feeling, a joke, an observation, a success, or an experience when it happens.

- Be gentle with yourself.

- Allow yourself to miss a day or more. Don't make journalizing a burden – life is hard enough.

- Keep it simple and easy for yourself – and on yourself. Even if what you want to write about your thoughts and feelings seems complicated, be brief and concise.

- Realize we all have hundreds of thousands of thoughts, feelings and images going through our minds daily. We cannot write them all down.

- Simply summarize the day in your Journal. A simple sentence can accomplish so much.

- If you already journal or want to start another journal with more information and detail, doing so can also support you.

- Use this Journal as a tool. Use it as an asset for growth, experience, expression, a tool for loving yourself, even laughing at yourself.

- Journaling can be work at times, even an obligation or a challenge, but it is only part of the process.

- Don't let such a process stop you, either because you don't recognize the process or feel the process is a burden. Move on; the moving on is the key to success.

- Change, a difference, can be just around the corner. Today does not have to look like yesterday or tomorrow.

# Using The Journal & Workbook Sections

## Under each heading, write in the lines provided
## for the current day and year until your Journal is full.

**20___ ___:** Write in the last two numbers of the current year on the two lines provided. For example – 20 _1_ _4_ for the year 2014, etc.

**Goals:** Your GOALS are your intentions and what you want to accomplish this year.

**Resolutions:** Your RESOLUTIONS are the actions and possible changes for how you are going to achieve what you want and reach your Goals.

**Monthly Focus Thought:** Before beginning each month of your Journal, on the lines provided for each year, summarize where you are and what you are feeling right then, that day. Keep it simple, one word, a few words, and a few sentences.

**January 1:** Here it is. The first line of journalizing the first day of your personal daily Journal. Because of the way The 5 Year Journal is designed, you can begin journaling on any day of the year. This will allow a reference and comparative look at the same date for the past years, up to 5 years. When this Journal is filled with your daily thoughts, you will have an accurate reflection of your experiences, thoughts and feelings over the previous 5 years of your life.

**Blank Pages:** Throughout the book there are places and pages that were intentionally left blank. Leave them blank, write in them, use them as scrapbook pages, it's up to you.

**Month End Summary:** Review your daily entries in order to summarize your overall experiences for that month.

**Quarterly Questions:** What Is My Favorite...? Have fun remembering what you did, saw, and felt. After your Favorite Movie or Favorite Song entry add the date, where you were, and (to enhance your memory) if anyone else was involved.

**Year End Questions:** What is My Favorite for the Year...? Re-read the Quarterly Questions and reflect back. Then write about all your overall Favorites for the year.

**The Best Thing That Happened To Me This Year Was...** Review all of your experiences for the year and write about what stood out the most, who or what effected you to the greatest extent, what or who you were the happiest about.

**The Worst Thing That Happened To Me This Year Was...** Review your entries and decide of all that happened – what was the hardest, most horrible, worst thing that you experienced.

**Q and A Year End:** Fill in the blanks by answering the questions provided, with how you felt and what you thought for the year.

**Create Your Own Topics:** Here is a place to create your own topic ideas, specific to your individual thoughts and personal interests.

**Year End Summary:** This is your year all wrapped up, with your overall thoughts and feelings. After reviewing this year's script of your life, and you get to review it.

**The 5 Year Journal Summary:** At the end of 5 years, summarize your overall experiences and feelings, what has happened to you and not happened, during the 5 years of this Journal.

# When You Start Your Journal

After the 20, write in the last two numbers of the current year
on the two lines that are provided.

For example… 20 __ __ …write in 14 for the year 2014, 15 for the year 2015, etc.

If you have not already done so, read the sections entitled —

- Introduction – The Purpose
- How To Use This Journal
- Using The Journal & Workbook Sections
- Doreene Clement's Reflections

**When you are ready to begin your journaling journey, the
5YJ can be started on any day of any year.**

**Easily summarize your day, create a gratitude journal, a health or diet journal,
and a prayer or dream journal, track your goals and intentions and so much
more, within these pages. If you want to journal more, use a blank book first
then come back to 5YJ.**

I created THE 5 YEAR JOURNAL through Divine Inspiration. That inspiration came in 1990, while I was driving in Phoenix, AZ. Such a simple, yet powerful idea, I thought it must be already out there. I looked and it wasn't. I first published 5YJ in 1999. It is a wonderful, amazing journal that shows up in people's lives, supporting, affirming, focusing and creating change for the better.

There were no other journals on the market, that I have seen, with all the features of 5YJ: in just minutes a day where you can journal daily for 5 years all in one book, with over 100 inspirational quotes, how-to journal instructions, and workbook sections – goals and resolutions, the best/worst thing that happened to me this year, year-end summary, create your own topics, monthly start and end focus thoughts, quarterly questions, year-end questions and so much more.

The real power within the pages of 5YJ is the actual journaling, with the advantage of only 3 lines per day: With the placement of each of the five years of journaling, one year after the last, right on the same page. As the user journals each year they can see where they were last year, two years, then three years ago, etc. And with the advantage of only three lines per day the user narrows down what was most important to them for that day. If they want to write more they can use a blank book to journal in first, and then come back to the 5YJ to summarize their day. 5YJ is also perfect to use for creating a gratitude journal, a prayer journal, or to track your goals and intentions. It has also been used by expectant mothers to journal to their child and then given as a gift to their child in later years. The uses are only limited by your imagination.

Doreene Clement

# Goals For The Year

20__ __ - _____

_____

20__ __ - _____

_____

20__ __ - _____

_____

20__ __ - _____

_____

20__ __ - _____

_____

*"Everything you are goes with you, everywhere you go."*

Doreene Clement

# Resolutions For The Year

20__ __ - _____

_____

20__ __ - _____

_____

20__ __ - _____

_____

20__ __ - _____

_____

20__ __ - _____

_____

# January Focus Thought

*Before beginning this month of your journal, on the lines provided for each year, summarize where you are and what you are feeling right then, that day. Keep it simple – one word, a few words, or a few short sentences.*

"I believe in the power of journaling. As a means of expression, journaling directly reveals to us the shadows of self."

Doreene Clement

20___ ___ - _____
_____
_____

20___ ___ - _____
_____
_____

20___ ___ - _____
_____
_____

20___ ___ - _____
_____
_____

20___ ___ - _____
_____
_____

## January 1

20__ __ - _____

_____

_____

20__ __ - _____

_____

_____

20__ __ - _____

_____

_____

20__ __ - _____

_____

_____

20__ __ - _____

_____

_____

*"The only man who never makes a mistake*

## January 2

20__ __ - _____

_____

_____

20__ __ - _____

_____

_____

20__ __ - _____

_____

_____

20__ __ - _____

_____

_____

20__ __ - _____

_____

_____

## January 3

20__ __ - _____

_____

_____

20__ __ - _____

_____

_____

20__ __ - _____

_____

_____

20__ __ - _____

_____

_____

20__ __ - _____

_____

_____

*…is the man who never does anything."*
*Theodore Roosevelt*

## January 4

20__ __ - _____

_____

_____

20__ __ - _____

_____

_____

20__ __ - _____

_____

_____

20__ __ - _____

_____

_____

20__ __ - _____

_____

_____

## January 5

20___ ___ - _____

_____

_____

20___ ___ - _____

_____

_____

20___ ___ - _____

_____

_____

20___ ___ - _____

_____

_____

20___ ___ - _____

_____

_____

*"Whatever I'm lacking – I'm not giving."*
Rita Davenport

## January 6

20___ ___ - _____

_____

_____

20___ ___ - _____

_____

_____

20___ ___ - _____

_____

_____

20___ ___ - _____

_____

_____

20___ ___ - _____

_____

_____

## January 7

20___ ___ - _____

_____

_____

20___ ___ - _____

_____

_____

20___ ___ - _____

_____

_____

20___ ___ - _____

_____

_____

20___ ___ - _____

_____

_____

*"Don't compromise yourself...you are all you've got."*
Janis Joplin

## January 8

20___ ___ - _____

_____

_____

20___ ___ - _____

_____

_____

20___ ___ - _____

_____

_____

20___ ___ - _____

_____

_____

20___ ___ - _____

_____

_____

# January 9

20__ __ - _____

_____

_____

20__ __ - _____

_____

_____

20__ __ - _____

_____

_____

20__ __ - _____

_____

_____

20__ __ - _____

_____

_____

*"Let your pen teach you what your soul already knows."*

Sue Meyn

# January 10

20__ __ - _____

_____

_____

20__ __ - _____

_____

_____

20__ __ - _____

_____

_____

20__ __ - _____

_____

_____

20__ __ - _____

_____

_____

## January 11

20__ __ - _____
_____
_____

20__ __ - _____
_____
_____

20__ __ - _____
_____
_____

20__ __ - _____
_____
_____

20__ __ - _____
_____
_____

*"I am never afraid of what I know."*
Anna Sewell

## January 12

20__ __ - _____
_____
_____

20__ __ - _____
_____
_____

20__ __ - _____
_____
_____

20__ __ - _____
_____
_____

20__ __ - _____
_____
_____

# January 13

20__ __ - _____

_____

_____

20__ __ - _____

_____

_____

20__ __ - _____

_____

_____

20__ __ - _____

_____

_____

20__ __ - _____

_____

_____

*"Never let your memories be greater than your dreams."*
Doug Ivester

# January 14

20__ __ - _____

_____

_____

20__ __ - _____

_____

_____

20__ __ - _____

_____

_____

20__ __ - _____

_____

_____

20__ __ - _____

_____

_____

## January 15

20__ __ - _____

_____

_____

20__ __ - _____

_____

_____

20__ __ - _____

_____

_____

20__ __ - _____

_____

_____

20__ __ - _____

_____

_____

*"I live in the present*

## January 16

20__ __ - _____

_____

_____

20__ __ - _____

_____

_____

20__ __ - _____

_____

_____

20__ __ - _____

_____

_____

20__ __ - _____

_____

_____

# January 17

20__ __ - _____

_____

_____

20__ __ - _____

_____

_____

20__ __ - _____

_____

_____

20__ __ - _____

_____

_____

20__ __ - _____

_____

_____

*...I only remember the past, and anticipate the future."*
Henry David Thoreau

# January 18

20__ __ - _____

_____

_____

20__ __ - _____

_____

_____

20__ __ - _____

_____

_____

20__ __ - _____

_____

_____

20__ __ - _____

_____

_____

## January 19

20__ __ - _____

_____

20__ __ - _____

_____

20__ __ - _____

_____

20__ __ - _____

_____

20__ __ - _____

_____

"You are never given a dream without
Theodore Roosevelt

## January 20

20__ __ - _____

_____

20__ __ - _____

_____

20__ __ - _____

_____

20__ __ - _____

_____

20__ __ - _____

_____

# January 21

20__ __ - _____

_____

20__ __ - _____

_____

20__ __ - _____

_____

20__ __ - _____

_____

20__ __ - _____

_____

*...also being given the power to make it true."*
*Richard Bach*

# January 22

20__ __ - _____

_____

20__ __ - _____

_____

20__ __ - _____

_____

20__ __ - _____

_____

20__ __ - _____

_____

## January 23

20__ __ - _____

_____

20__ __ - _____

_____

20__ __ - _____

_____

20__ __ - _____

_____

20__ __ - _____

_____

*"The richest people in the world look for and build*

## January 24

20__ __ - _____

_____

20__ __ - _____

_____

20__ __ - _____

_____

20__ __ - _____

_____

20__ __ - _____

_____

## January 25

20__ __ - _____

_____

_____

20__ __ - _____

_____

_____

20__ __ - _____

_____

_____

20__ __ - _____

_____

_____

20__ __ - _____

_____

_____

*...networks. Everyone else looks for work."*
*Robert Kiyosaki*

## January 26

20__ __ - _____

_____

_____

20__ __ - _____

_____

_____

20__ __ - _____

_____

_____

20__ __ - _____

_____

_____

20__ __ - _____

_____

_____

## January 27

20__ __ - _____

_____

_____

20__ __ - _____

_____

_____

20__ __ - _____

_____

_____

20__ __ - _____

_____

_____

20__ __ - _____

_____

_____

*"That's when I finally understood that the problem*

## January 28

20__ __ - _____

_____

_____

20__ __ - _____

_____

_____

20__ __ - _____

_____

_____

20__ __ - _____

_____

_____

20__ __ - _____

_____

_____

## January 29

20__ __ - _____

_____

_____

20__ __ - _____

_____

_____

20__ __ - _____

_____

_____

20__ __ - _____

_____

_____

20__ __ - _____

_____

_____

*…wasn't 'it' – the problem was 'me'."*
Jim Rohn

## January 30

20__ __ - _____

_____

_____

20__ __ - _____

_____

_____

20__ __ - _____

_____

_____

20__ __ - _____

_____

_____

20__ __ - _____

_____

_____

# January 31

20__ __ - _____

_____

20__ __ - _____

_____

20__ __ - _____

_____

20__ __ - _____

_____

20__ __ - _____

_____

*"Get outside of the moment to live in the Now."*
Dehbra Taylor

# January Month End Summary

20__ __ - _____

_____

20__ __ - _____

_____

20__ __ - _____

_____

20__ __ - _____

_____

20__ __ - _____

_____

# Notes, Thoughts, Doodles, Ideas

# February Focus Thought

*Before beginning this month of your journal, on the lines provided for each year, summarize where you are and what you are feeling right then, that day. Keep it simple – one word, a few words, or a few short sentences.*

"Life's moments are individual, custom-made opportunities, tailored just for me to learn my lessons well. Those moments are a potential for growth and peace. In my core, I know that this is all real and true. I don't always remember to live by these beliefs, but I do always come back to them."

Doreene Clement

20__ __ - _____
_____
_____

20__ __ - _____
_____
_____

20__ __ - _____
_____
_____

20__ __ - _____
_____
_____

20__ __ - _____
_____
_____

## February 1

20__ __ - _____
_____
_____

20__ __ - _____
_____
_____

20__ __ - _____
_____
_____

20__ __ - _____
_____
_____

20__ __ - _____
_____
_____

*"Nothing can bring you peace but yourself."*
Ralph Waldo Emerson

## February 2

20__ __ - _____
_____
_____

20__ __ - _____
_____
_____

20__ __ - _____
_____
_____

20__ __ - _____
_____
_____

20__ __ - _____
_____
_____

# February 3

20___ ___ - _____

_____

20___ ___ - _____

_____

20___ ___ - _____

_____

20___ ___ - _____

_____

20___ ___ - _____

_____

"To confine our attention to terrestrial matters

# February 4

20___ ___ - _____

_____

20___ ___ - _____

_____

20___ ___ - _____

_____

20___ ___ - _____

_____

20___ ___ - _____

_____

## February 5

20__ __ - _____

_____

_____

20__ __ - _____

_____

_____

20__ __ - _____

_____

_____

20__ __ - _____

_____

_____

20__ __ - _____

_____

_____

…would be to limit the human spirit."
Stephen Hawking

## February 6

20__ __ - _____

_____

_____

20__ __ - _____

_____

_____

20__ __ - _____

_____

_____

20__ __ - _____

_____

_____

20__ __ - _____

_____

_____

# February 7

20__ __ - _____

_____

20__ __ - _____

_____

20__ __ - _____

_____

20__ __ - _____

_____

20__ __ - _____

_____

*"Some men see things as they are and say 'Why?"*

# February 8

20__ __ - _____

_____

20__ __ - _____

_____

20__ __ - _____

_____

20__ __ - _____

_____

20__ __ - _____

_____

## February 9

20__ __ - _____

_____

_____

20__ __ - _____

_____

_____

20__ __ - _____

_____

_____

20__ __ - _____

_____

_____

20__ __ - _____

_____

_____

*...I dream things that never were, and say 'Why not?'*
*George Bernard Shaw*

## February 10

20__ __ - _____

_____

_____

20__ __ - _____

_____

_____

20__ __ - _____

_____

_____

20__ __ - _____

_____

_____

20__ __ - _____

_____

_____

# February 11

20__ __ - _____

_____

_____

20__ __ - _____

_____

_____

20__ __ - _____

_____

_____

20__ __ - _____

_____

_____

20__ __ - _____

_____

_____

*"When you have purpose, you don't have time for negativity."*
Mark Victor Hansen

# February 12

20__ __ - _____

_____

_____

20__ __ - _____

_____

_____

20__ __ - _____

_____

_____

20__ __ - _____

_____

_____

20__ __ - _____

_____

_____

# February 13

20__ __ - _____

_____

_____

20__ __ - _____

_____

_____

20__ __ - _____

_____

_____

20__ __ - _____

_____

_____

20__ __ - _____

_____

_____

*"Light tomorrow with today!"*
*Elizabeth Barrett Browning*

# February 14

20__ __ - _____

_____

_____

20__ __ - _____

_____

_____

20__ __ - _____

_____

_____

20__ __ - _____

_____

_____

20__ __ - _____

_____

_____

# February 15

20___ ___ - _____

_____

20___ ___ - _____

_____

20___ ___ - _____

_____

20___ ___ - _____

_____

20___ ___ - _____

_____

*"Find a place inside where there is joy*

# February 16

20___ ___ - _____

_____

20___ ___ - _____

_____

20___ ___ - _____

_____

20___ ___ - _____

_____

20___ ___ - _____

_____

# February 17

20__ __ - _____
_____
_____

20__ __ - _____
_____
_____

20__ __ - _____
_____
_____

20__ __ - _____
_____
_____

20__ __ - _____
_____
_____

...and the joy will burn out the pain."
Joseph Campbell

# February 18

20__ __ - _____
_____
_____

20__ __ - _____
_____
_____

20__ __ - _____
_____
_____

20__ __ - _____
_____
_____

20__ __ - _____
_____
_____

# February 19

20__ __ - _____

_____

_____

20__ __ - _____

_____

_____

20__ __ - _____

_____

_____

20__ __ - _____

_____

_____

20__ __ - _____

_____

_____

*"Walk your path with dancing feet and a song in your heart."*
Ariel Wolfe

# February 20

20__ __ - _____

_____

_____

20__ __ - _____

_____

_____

20__ __ - _____

_____

_____

20__ __ - _____

_____

_____

20__ __ - _____

_____

_____

# February 21

20__ __ - _____

_____

_____

20__ __ - _____

_____

_____

20__ __ - _____

_____

_____

20__ __ - _____

_____

_____

20__ __ - _____

_____

_____

*"Nobody can make you feel inferior without your permission."*
Eleanor Roosevelt

# February 22

20__ __ - _____

_____

_____

20__ __ - _____

_____

_____

20__ __ - _____

_____

_____

20__ __ - _____

_____

_____

20__ __ - _____

_____

_____

# February 23

20___ ___ - _____

_____

20___ ___ - _____

_____

20___ ___ - _____

_____

20___ ___ - _____

_____

20___ ___ - _____

_____

"Let go of everything not divinely designed for me,

# February 24

20___ ___ - _____

_____

20___ ___ - _____

_____

20___ ___ - _____

_____

20___ ___ - _____

_____

20___ ___ - _____

_____

# February 25

20__ __ - _____

_____

_____

20__ __ - _____

_____

_____

20__ __ - _____

_____

_____

20__ __ - _____

_____

_____

20__ __ - _____

_____

_____

*...and the perfect plan of my life comes to pass."*
*Florence Scoville Shinn*

# February 26

20__ __ - _____

_____

_____

20__ __ - _____

_____

_____

20__ __ - _____

_____

_____

20__ __ - _____

_____

_____

20__ __ - _____

_____

_____

## February 27

20___ ___ - _____

_____

_____

20___ ___ - _____

_____

_____

20___ ___ - _____

_____

_____

20___ ___ - _____

_____

_____

20___ ___ - _____

_____

_____

*"Assume the feeling of the wish fulfilled."*
Pierre O'Rourke

## February 28

20___ ___ - _____

_____

_____

20___ ___ - _____

_____

_____

20___ ___ - _____

_____

_____

20___ ___ - _____

_____

_____

20___ ___ - _____

_____

_____

# February 29

20__ __ - _____

_____

_____

20__ __ - _____

_____

_____

20__ __ - _____

_____

_____

20__ __ - _____

_____

_____

20__ __ - _____

_____

_____

*"I am enough because I exist."*
Rev. Karen Russo

# February Month End Summary

20__ __ - _____

_____

_____

20__ __ - _____

_____

_____

20__ __ - _____

_____

_____

20__ __ - _____

_____

_____

20__ __ - _____

_____

_____

# March Focus Thought

*Before beginning this month of your journal, on the lines provided for each year, summarize where you are and what you are feeling right then, that day. Keep it simple – one word, a few words, or a few short sentences.*

"Where we go within our minds and with our actions, what we do with all of our daily experiences, determines our degree of peace and joy, our happiness

...or our sorrow, loss, and pain."

Doreene Clement

20__ __ - _____

_____

20__ __ - _____

_____

20__ __ - _____

_____

20__ __ - _____

_____

20__ __ - _____

_____

## March 1

20__ __ - _____

_____

20__ __ - _____

_____

20__ __ - _____

_____

20__ __ - _____

_____

20__ __ - _____

_____

*"All events on this planet are neutral events,*

## March 2

20__ __ - _____

_____

20__ __ - _____

_____

20__ __ - _____

_____

20__ __ - _____

_____

20__ __ - _____

_____

# March 3

20__ __ - _____
_____
_____

20__ __ - _____
_____
_____

20__ __ - _____
_____
_____

20__ __ - _____
_____
_____

20__ __ - _____
_____
_____

...except for the emotion we assign them."
Melinda Vail

# March 4

20__ __ - _____
_____
_____

20__ __ - _____
_____
_____

20__ __ - _____
_____
_____

20__ __ - _____
_____
_____

20__ __ - _____
_____
_____

## March 5

20___ ___ - _____

_____

20___ ___ - _____

_____

20___ ___ - _____

_____

20___ ___ - _____

_____

20___ ___ - _____

_____

*"I long to accomplish a great and noble task,*

## March 6

20___ ___ - _____

_____

20___ ___ - _____

_____

20___ ___ - _____

_____

20___ ___ - _____

_____

20___ ___ - _____

_____

## March 7

20__ __ - _____

_____

_____

20__ __ - _____

_____

_____

20__ __ - _____

_____

_____

20__ __ - _____

_____

_____

20__ __ - _____

_____

_____

…but it is my chief duty to accomplish small tasks

## March 8

20__ __ - _____

_____

_____

20__ __ - _____

_____

_____

20__ __ - _____

_____

_____

20__ __ - _____

_____

_____

20__ __ - _____

_____

_____

## March 9

20__ __ - _____

_____

_____

20__ __ - _____

_____

_____

20__ __ - _____

_____

_____

20__ __ - _____

_____

_____

20__ __ - _____

_____

_____

...as if they were great and noble."
Helen Keller

## March 10

20__ __ - _____

_____

_____

20__ __ - _____

_____

_____

20__ __ - _____

_____

_____

20__ __ - _____

_____

20__ __ - _____

_____

_____

## March 11

20__ __ - _____

_____

20__ __ - _____

_____

20__ __ - _____

_____

20__ __ - _____

_____

20__ __ - _____

_____

_____

"It isn't what you have, or who you are, or where you are,

## March 12

20__ __ - _____

_____

20__ __ - _____

_____

20__ __ - _____

_____

20__ __ - _____

_____

20__ __ - _____

_____

_____

## March 13

20___ ___ - _____

_____

20___ ___ - _____

_____

20___ ___ - _____

_____

20___ ___ - _____

_____

20___ ___ - _____

_____

*...or what you are doing that makes you happy*

## March 14

20___ ___ - _____

_____

20___ ___ - _____

_____

20___ ___ - _____

_____

20___ ___ - _____

_____

20___ ___ - _____

_____

# March 15

20__ __ - _____

_____

_____

20__ __ - _____

_____

_____

20__ __ - _____

_____

_____

20__ __ - _____

_____

_____

20__ __ - _____

_____

_____

...or unhappy. It is what you think about."
Dale Carnegie

# March 16

20__ __ - _____

_____

_____

20__ __ - _____

_____

_____

20__ __ - _____

_____

_____

20__ __ - _____

_____

_____

20__ __ - _____

_____

_____

# March 17

20__ __ - _____

_____

20__ __ - _____

_____

20__ __ - _____

_____

20__ __ - _____

_____

20__ __ - _____

_____

*"Learn how to feel joy."*
Seneca

# March 18

20__ __ - _____

_____

20__ __ - _____

_____

20__ __ - _____

_____

20__ __ - _____

_____

20__ __ - _____

_____

## March 19

20__ __ - _____
_____
_____

20__ __ - _____
_____
_____

20__ __ - _____
_____
_____

20__ __ - _____
_____
_____

20__ __ - _____
_____
_____

*"When I was younger*

## March 20

20__ __ - _____
_____
_____

20__ __ - _____
_____
_____

20__ __ - _____
_____
_____

20__ __ - _____
_____
_____

20__ __ - _____
_____
_____

## March 21

20__ __ - _____

_____

_____

20__ __ - _____

_____

_____

20__ __ - _____

_____

_____

20__ __ - _____

_____

_____

20__ __ - _____

_____

_____

*…I could remember anything*

## March 22

20__ __ - _____

_____

_____

20__ __ - _____

_____

_____

20__ __ - _____

_____

_____

20__ __ - _____

_____

_____

20__ __ - _____

_____

_____

## March 23

20__ __ - _____

_____

_____

20__ __ - _____

_____

_____

20__ __ - _____

_____

_____

20__ __ - _____

_____

_____

20__ __ - _____

_____

_____

*…whether it happened or not."*
Mark Twain

## March 24

20__ __ - _____

_____

_____

20__ __ - _____

_____

_____

20__ __ - _____

_____

_____

20__ __ - _____

_____

_____

20__ __ - _____

_____

_____

# March 25

20__ __ - _____

_____

_____

20__ __ - _____

_____

_____

20__ __ - _____

_____

_____

20__ __ - _____

_____

_____

20__ __ - _____

_____

_____

*"Don't let life bring you down, bring life up."*
Erin Rose Bunzel

# March 26

20__ __ - _____

_____

20__ __ - _____

_____

20__ __ - _____

_____

20__ __ - _____

_____

20__ __ - _____

_____

_____

## March 27

20__ __ - _____
_____
_____

20__ __ - _____
_____
_____

20__ __ - _____
_____
_____

20__ __ - _____
_____
_____

20__ __ - _____
_____
_____

"The key is to keep company only with

## March 28

20__ __ - _____
_____
_____

20__ __ - _____
_____
_____

20__ __ - _____
_____

20__ __ - _____
_____

20__ __ - _____
_____
_____

## March 29

20__ __ - _____

_____

20__ __ - _____

_____

20__ __ - _____

_____

20__ __ - _____

_____

20__ __ - _____

_____

*...people who uplift you, whose*

## March 30

20__ __ - _____

_____

20__ __ - _____

_____

20__ __ - _____

_____

20__ __ - _____

_____

20__ __ - _____

_____

# March 31

20__ __ - _____

_____

20__ __ - _____

_____

20__ __ - _____

_____

20__ __ - _____

_____

20__ __ - _____

_____

*...presence calls forth your best."*
*Epictetus*

# March Month End Summary

20__ __ - _____

_____

20__ __ - _____

_____

20__ __ - _____

_____

20__ __ - _____

_____

20__ __ - _____

_____

# Year 1 – First Quarter Highlights
## January thru March 20 __ __

## What Was My Favorite...

Adventure_____

Book I Read _____

Day _____

Dream_____

Event_____

Exercise_____

Experience_____

Family Moment_____

Gift Given_____

Gift Received_____

Idea_____

Lesson_____

Meal_____

Movie_____

Person_____

Quote_____

Reflection_____

Relaxation_____

Song_____

Spiritual Moment_____

Success_____

Thought_____

TV Show_____

Volunteering_____

Wish _____

Other _____

Other _____

Other _____

## Year 2 – First Quarter Highlights
## January thru March 20 __ __

## What Was My Favorite...

Adventure_____

Book I Read _____

Day _____

Dream _____

Event _____

Exercise_____

Experience_____

Family Moment_____

Gift Given_____

Gift Received_____

Idea_____

Lesson_____

Meal_____

Movie_____

Person_____

Quote_____

Reflection_____

Relaxation_____

Song_____

Spiritual Moment_____

Success_____

Thought_____

TV Show_____

Volunteering_____

Wish _____

Other _____

Other _____

Other _____

# Year 3 – First Quarter Highlights
## January thru March 20 __ __

## What Was My Favorite…

Adventure_____

Book I Read _____

Day _____

Dream_____

Event_____

Exercise_____

Experience_____

Family Moment_____

Gift Given_____

Gift Received_____

Idea_____

Lesson_____

Meal_____

Movie_____

Person_____

Quote_____

Reflection_____

Relaxation_____

Song_____

Spiritual Moment_____

Success_____

Thought_____

TV Show_____

Volunteering_____

Wish _____

Other _____

Other _____

Other _____

## Year 4 – First Quarter Highlights
## January thru March 20 __ __

## What Was My Favorite...

Adventure_____

Book I Read _____

Day _____

Dream_____

Event_____

Exercise_____

Experience_____

Family Moment_____

Gift Given_____

Gift Received_____

Idea_____

Lesson_____

Meal_____

Movie_____

Person_____

Quote_____

Reflection_____

Relaxation_____

Song_____

Spiritual Moment_____

Success_____

Thought_____

TV Show_____

Volunteering_____

Wish _____

Other _____

Other _____

Other _____

## Year 5 – First Quarter Highlights
## January thru March 20 __ __

## What Was My Favorite...

Adventure_____

Book I Read _____

Day _____

Dream_____

Event_____

Exercise_____

Experience_____

Family Moment_____

Gift Given_____

Gift Received_____

Idea_____

Lesson_____

Meal_____

Movie_____

Person_____

Quote_____

Reflection_____

Relaxation_____

Song_____

Spiritual Moment_____

Success_____

Thought_____

TV Show_____

Volunteering_____

Wish _____

Other _____

Other _____

Other _____

# April Focus Thought

*Before beginning this month of your journal, on the lines provided for each year, summarize where you are and what you are feeling right then, that day. Keep it simple – one word, a few words, or a few short sentences.*

"I have the confirmed belief that each of life's moments holds a purpose and a gift. I don't always remember to live by these beliefs, but I do always come back to them."

Doreene Clement

20__ __ - _____

_____

20__ __ - _____

_____

20__ __ - _____

_____

20__ __ - _____

_____

20__ __ - _____

_____

# April 1

20__ __ - _____

_____

20__ __ - _____

_____

20__ __ - _____

_____

20__ __ - _____

_____

20__ __ - _____

_____

"Never underestimate the power of dreams

# April 2

20__ __ - _____

_____

20__ __ - _____

_____

20__ __ - _____

_____

20__ __ - _____

_____

20__ __ - _____

_____

## April 3

20___ ___ - _____

_____

_____

20___ ___ - _____

_____

_____

20___ ___ - _____

_____

_____

20___ ___ - _____

_____

_____

20___ ___ - _____

_____

_____

...and the influence of the human spirit.

## April 4

20___ ___ - _____

_____

_____

20___ ___ - _____

_____

_____

20___ ___ - _____

_____

_____

20___ ___ - _____

_____

_____

20___ ___ - _____

_____

_____

# April 5

20__ __ - _____

_____

_____

20__ __ - _____

_____

_____

20__ __ - _____

_____

_____

20__ __ - _____

_____

_____

20__ __ - _____

_____

_____

…We are all the same in this notion: The potential

# April 6

20__ __ - _____

_____

_____

20__ __ - _____

_____

_____

20__ __ - _____

_____

_____

20__ __ - _____

_____

_____

20__ __ - _____

_____

_____

# April 7

20___ ___ - _____
_____
_____

20___ ___ - _____
_____
_____

20___ ___ - _____
_____
_____

20___ ___ - _____
_____
_____

20___ ___ - _____
_____
_____

...for greatness lives within each of us."
Wilma Glodean Rudolph

# April 8

20___ ___ - _____
_____
_____

20___ ___ - _____
_____
_____

20___ ___ - _____
_____
_____

20___ ___ - _____
_____
_____

20___ ___ - _____
_____
_____

# April 9

20__ __ - _____

_____

20__ __ - _____

_____

20__ __ - _____

_____

20__ __ - _____

_____

20__ __ - _____

_____

"One today is worth two tomorrows."
Benjamin Franklin

# April 10

20__ __ - _____

_____

20__ __ - _____

_____

20__ __ - _____

_____

20__ __ - _____

_____

20__ __ - _____

_____

# April 11

20__ __ - _____

_____

20__ __ - _____

_____

20__ __ - _____

_____

20__ __ - _____

_____

20__ __ - _____

_____

"Educating the mind without educating

# April 12

20__ __ - _____

_____

20__ __ - _____

_____

20__ __ - _____

_____

20__ __ - _____

_____

20__ __ - _____

_____

# April 13

20__ __ - _____

_____

_____

20__ __ - _____

_____

_____

20__ __ - _____

_____

_____

20__ __ - _____

_____

_____

20__ __ - _____

_____

_____

*...the heart is no education at all."*
*Aristotle*

# April 14

20__ __ - _____

_____

_____

20__ __ - _____

_____

_____

20__ __ - _____

_____

_____

20__ __ - _____

_____

_____

20__ __ - _____

_____

_____

# April 15

20__ __ - _____

_____

20__ __ - _____

_____

20__ __ - _____

_____

20__ __ - _____

_____

20__ __ - _____

_____

"Remember, what you believe

# April 16

20__ __ - _____

_____

20__ __ - _____

_____

20__ __ - _____

_____

20__ __ - _____

_____

20__ __ - _____

_____

# April 17

20__ __ - _____

_____

20__ __ - _____

_____

20__ __ - _____

_____

20__ __ - _____

_____

20__ __ - _____

_____

…and say to yourself,

# April 18

20__ __ - _____

_____

20__ __ - _____

_____

20__ __ - _____

_____

20__ __ - _____

_____

20__ __ - _____

_____

# April 19

20__ __ - _____
_____
_____

20__ __ - _____
_____
_____

20__ __ - _____
_____
_____

20__ __ - _____
_____
_____

20__ __ - _____
_____
_____

*…manifests into reality."*
Dr. John Demartini

# April 20

20__ __ - _____
_____
_____

20__ __ - _____
_____
_____

20__ __ - _____
_____
_____

20__ __ - _____
_____
_____

20__ __ - _____
_____
_____

# April 21

20__ __ - _____

_____

20__ __ - _____

_____

20__ __ - _____

_____

20__ __ - _____

_____

20__ __ - _____

_____

*"Even death is not to be feared by one who has lived wisely."*
Buddha

# April 22

20__ __ - _____

_____

20__ __ - _____

_____

20__ __ - _____

_____

20__ __ - _____

_____

20__ __ - _____

_____

# April 23

20__ __ - _____

_____

20__ __ - _____

_____

20__ __ - _____

_____

20__ __ - _____

_____

20__ __ - _____

_____

"Many are stubborn in pursuit of the path they have chosen,

# April 24

20__ __ - _____

_____

20__ __ - _____

_____

20__ __ - _____

_____

20__ __ - _____

_____

20__ __ - _____

_____

# April 25

20__ __ - _____

_____

_____

20__ __ - _____

_____

_____

20__ __ - _____

_____

_____

20__ __ - _____

_____

_____

20__ __ - _____

_____

_____

*...few in pursuit of the goal."*
*Friedrich Nietzche*

# April 26

20__ __ - _____

_____

_____

20__ __ - _____

_____

_____

20__ __ - _____

_____

_____

20__ __ - _____

_____

_____

20__ __ - _____

_____

_____

## April 27

20__ __ - _____

_____

20__ __ - _____

_____

20__ __ - _____

_____

20__ __ - _____

_____

20__ __ - _____

_____

*"Wherever there is a human being,*

## April 28

20__ __ - _____

_____

20__ __ - _____

_____

20__ __ - _____

_____

20__ __ - _____

_____

20__ __ - _____

_____

# April 29

20__ __ - _____

_____

20__ __ - _____

_____

20__ __ - _____

_____

20__ __ - _____

_____

20__ __ - _____

_____

…that is happiness."
Lucius Annaeus Seneca

# April 30

20__ __ - _____

_____

20__ __ - _____

_____

20__ __ - _____

_____

20__ __ - _____

_____

# April Month End Summary

20__ __ - _____
_____
_____

20__ __ - _____
_____
_____

20__ __ - _____
_____
_____

20__ __ - _____
_____
_____

20__ __ - _____
_____
_____

"Action expresses priorities."
Mahatma Gandhi

# Notes, Thoughts, Doodles, Ideas

# May Focus Thought

*Before beginning this month of your journal, on the lines provided for each year, summarize where you are and what you are feeling right then, that day. Keep it simple – one word, a few words, or a few short sentences.*

"There are no accidents. Nothing is random. Life's lessons come hand in hand with their opportunities.

The lesson was about realizing, knowing with every breath and every beat of my heart, that I am Blessed. We All Are."

Doreene Clement

20__ __ - _____

_____

_____

20__ __ - _____

_____

_____

20__ __ - _____

_____

_____

20__ __ - _____

_____

_____

20__ __ - _____

_____

_____

## May 1

20__ __ - _____

_____

_____

20__ __ - _____

_____

_____

20__ __ - _____

_____

_____

20__ __ - _____

_____

_____

20__ __ - _____

_____

_____

"It doesn't matter where you are coming from. All

## May 2

20__ __ - _____

_____

_____

20__ __ - _____

_____

_____

20__ __ - _____

_____

_____

20__ __ - _____

_____

_____

20__ __ - _____

_____

_____

## May 3

20___ ___ - _____

_____

_____

20___ ___ - _____

_____

_____

20___ ___ - _____

_____

_____

20___ ___ - _____

_____

_____

20___ ___ - _____

_____

_____

*...that matters is where you are going."*
Brian Tracy

## May 4

20___ ___ - _____

_____

_____

20___ ___ - _____

_____

_____

20___ ___ - _____

_____

_____

20___ ___ - _____

_____

_____

20___ ___ - _____

_____

_____

## May 5

20__ __ - _____

_____

_____

20__ __ - _____

_____

_____

20__ __ - _____

_____

_____

20__ __ - _____

_____

_____

20__ __ - _____

_____

_____

*"Live out of your imagination, not your history."*
Dr. Stephen Covey

## May 6

20__ __ - _____

_____

_____

20__ __ - _____

_____

_____

20__ __ - _____

_____

_____

20__ __ - _____

_____

_____

20__ __ - _____

_____

_____

# May 7

20__ __ - _____

_____

20__ __ - _____

_____

20__ __ - _____

_____

20__ __ - _____

_____

20__ __ - _____

_____

"Every moment and every event of every man's life

# May 8

20__ __ - _____

_____

20__ __ - _____

_____

20__ __ - _____

_____

20__ __ - _____

_____

20__ __ - _____

_____

## May 9

20__ __ - _____

_____

20__ __ - _____

_____

20__ __ - _____

_____

20__ __ - _____

_____

20__ __ - _____

_____

*…on earth plants something in his soul."*
*Thomas Merton*

## May 10

20__ __ - _____

_____

20__ __ - _____

_____

20__ __ - _____

_____

20__ __ - _____

_____

20__ __ - _____

_____

## May 11

20__ __ - _____

_____

20__ __ - _____

_____

20__ __ - _____

_____

20__ __ - _____

_____

20__ __ - _____

_____

"Of all the music that reached farthest into heaven,

## May 12

20__ __ - _____

_____

20__ __ - _____

_____

20__ __ - _____

_____

20__ __ - _____

_____

20__ __ - _____

_____

## May 13

20__ __ - _____

_____

20__ __ - _____

_____

20__ __ - _____

_____

20__ __ - _____

_____

20__ __ - _____

_____

…it is the beating of a loving heart."
Henry Ward Beecher

## May 14

20__ __ - _____

_____

20__ __ - _____

_____

20__ __ - _____

_____

20__ __ - _____

_____

20__ __ - _____

_____

**May 15**

20___ ___ - _____

_____

20___ ___ - _____

_____

20___ ___ - _____

_____

20___ ___ - _____

_____

20___ ___ - _____

_____

"A man who dares to waste one hour of time

**May 16**

20___ ___ - _____

_____

20___ ___ - _____

_____

20___ ___ - _____

_____

20___ ___ - _____

_____

20___ ___ - _____

_____

## May 17

20___ ___ - _____

_____

20___ ___ - _____

_____

20___ ___ - _____

_____

20___ ___ - _____

_____

20___ ___ - _____

_____

*...has not discovered the value of life."*
*Charles Darwin*

## May 18

20___ ___ - _____

_____

20___ ___ - _____

_____

20___ ___ - _____

_____

20___ ___ - _____

_____

20___ ___ - _____

_____

## May 19

20__ __ - _____

_____

20__ __ - _____

_____

20__ __ - _____

_____

20__ __ - _____

_____

20__ __ - _____

_____

*"Virtue is bold, and goodness never fearful."*
William Shakespeare

## May 20

20__ __ - _____

_____

20__ __ - _____

_____

20__ __ - _____

_____

20__ __ - _____

_____

20__ __ - _____

_____

## May 21

20__ __ - _____

_____

20__ __ - _____

_____

20__ __ - _____

_____

20__ __ - _____

_____

20__ __ - _____

_____

*"It always seems impossible until it is done."*
Nelson Mandela

## May 22

20__ __ - _____

_____

20__ __ - _____

_____

20__ __ - _____

_____

20__ __ - _____

_____

20__ __ - _____

_____

## May 23

20__ __ - _____

_____

20__ __ - _____

_____

20__ __ - _____

_____

20__ __ - _____

_____

20__ __ - _____

_____

"Failure seldom stops you;

## May 24

20__ __ - _____

_____

20__ __ - _____

_____

20__ __ - _____

_____

20__ __ - _____

_____

20__ __ - _____

_____

## May 25

20__ __ - _____

_____

_____

20__ __ - _____

_____

_____

20__ __ - _____

_____

_____

20__ __ - _____

_____

_____

20__ __ - _____

_____

_____

*…what stops you is the fear of failure."*
*Jack Lemmon*

## May 26

20__ __ - _____

_____

_____

20__ __ - _____

_____

_____

20__ __ - _____

_____

_____

20__ __ - _____

_____

_____

20__ __ - _____

_____

_____

## May 27

20__ __ - _____

_____

20__ __ - _____

_____

20__ __ - _____

_____

20__ __ - _____

_____

20__ __ - _____

_____

*"Always do your best. What*

## May 28

20__ __ - _____

_____

20__ __ - _____

_____

20__ __ - _____

_____

20__ __ - _____

_____

20__ __ - _____

_____

**May 29**

20___ ___ - _____

_____

20___ ___ - _____

_____

20___ ___ - _____

_____

20___ ___ - _____

_____

20___ ___ - _____

_____

...you plant now, you will harvest later."
Og Mandino

**May 30**

20___ ___ - _____

_____

20___ ___ - _____

_____

20___ ___ - _____

_____

20___ ___ - _____

_____

20___ ___ - _____

_____

## May 31

20__ __ - _____

_____

20__ __ - _____

_____

20__ __ - _____

_____

20__ __ - _____

_____

20__ __ - _____

_____

*"Love is the flower you have got to let grow."*
John Lennon

## May Month End Summary

20__ __ - _____

_____

20__ __ - _____

_____

20__ __ - _____

_____

20__ __ - _____

_____

20__ __ - _____

_____

# Notes, Thoughts, Doodles, Ideas

# June Focus Thought

*Before beginning this month of your journal, on the lines provided for each year, summarize where you are and what you are feeling right then, that day. Keep it simple – one word, a few words, or a few short sentences.*

"The lesson was about realizing, knowing with every breath and every beat of my heart, that I Am So Blessed. We All Are."

Doreene Clement

20__ __ - _____
_____

20__ __ - _____
_____

20__ __ - _____
_____

20__ __ - _____
_____

20__ __ - _____
_____

# June 1

20__ __ - _____

_____

_____

20__ __ - _____

_____

_____

20__ __ - _____

_____

_____

20__ __ - _____

_____

_____

20__ __ - _____

_____

_____

"Every saint has a past, and every sinner has a future."
Oscar Wilde

# June 2

20__ __ - _____

_____

_____

20__ __ - _____

_____

_____

20__ __ - _____

_____

_____

20__ __ - _____

_____

_____

20__ __ - _____

_____

_____

## June 3

20___ ___ - _____

_____

20___ ___ - _____

_____

20___ ___ - _____

_____

20___ ___ - _____

_____

20___ ___ - _____

_____

*"We may encounter many defeats*

## June 4

20___ ___ - _____

_____

20___ ___ - _____

_____

20___ ___ - _____

_____

20___ ___ - _____

_____

20___ ___ - _____

_____

## June 5

20__ __ - _____

_____

20__ __ - _____

_____

20__ __ - _____

_____

20__ __ - _____

_____

20__ __ - _____

_____

*…but we must not be defeated."*
Maya Angelou

## June 6

20__ __ - _____

_____

20__ __ - _____

_____

20__ __ - _____

_____

20__ __ - _____

_____

20__ __ - _____

_____

# June 7

20__ __ - _____

_____

_____

20__ __ - _____

_____

_____

20__ __ - _____

_____

_____

20__ __ - _____

_____

_____

20__ __ - _____

_____

_____

*"If you learn from defeat,"*

# June 8

20__ __ - _____

_____

_____

20__ __ - _____

_____

_____

20__ __ - _____

_____

_____

20__ __ - _____

_____

_____

20__ __ - _____

_____

_____

## June 9

20__ __ - _____

_____

_____

20__ __ - _____

_____

_____

20__ __ - _____

_____

_____

20__ __ - _____

_____

_____

20__ __ - _____

_____

_____

*…you haven't really lost."*
*Zig Ziglar*

## June 10

20__ __ - _____

_____

_____

20__ __ - _____

_____

_____

20__ __ - _____

_____

_____

20__ __ - _____

_____

_____

20__ __ - _____

_____

_____

## June 11

20__ __ - _____

_____

20__ __ - _____

_____

20__ __ - _____

_____

20__ __ - _____

_____

20__ __ - _____

_____

"Truth is exact

## June 12

20__ __ - _____

_____

20__ __ - _____

_____

20__ __ - _____

_____

20__ __ - _____

_____

20__ __ - _____

_____

# June 13

20__ __ - _____

_____

20__ __ - _____

_____

20__ __ - _____

_____

20__ __ - _____

_____

20__ __ - _____

_____

*...correspondence with reality."*
Paramahansa Yogananda

# June 14

20__ __ - _____

_____

20__ __ - _____

_____

20__ __ - _____

_____

20__ __ - _____

_____

20__ __ - _____

_____

## June 15

20__ __ - _____

_____

20__ __ - _____

_____

20__ __ - _____

_____

20__ __ - _____

_____

20__ __ - _____

_____

"To grow is to change. The only thing constant is change.

## June 16

20__ __ - _____

_____

20__ __ - _____

_____

20__ __ - _____

_____

20__ __ - _____

_____

20__ __ - _____

_____

# June 17

20__ __ - _____

_____

20__ __ - _____

_____

20__ __ - _____

_____

20__ __ - _____

_____

20__ __ - _____

_____

*...Therefore, to have changed often is to have grown much."*
*Sandy Rogers*

# June 18

20__ __ - _____

_____

20__ __ - _____

_____

20__ __ - _____

_____

20__ __ - _____

_____

20__ __ - _____

_____

## June 19

20__ __ - _____

_____

20__ __ - _____

_____

20__ __ - _____

_____

20__ __ - _____

_____

20__ __ - _____

_____

*"I tell you, we are here on Earth to fart around,*

## June 20

20__ __ - _____

_____

20__ __ - _____

_____

20__ __ - _____

_____

20__ __ - _____

_____

20__ __ - _____

_____

# June 21

20__ __ - _____

_____

20__ __ - _____

_____

20__ __ - _____

_____

20__ __ - _____

_____

20__ __ - _____

_____

*...and don't let anybody tell you different."*
*Kurt Vonnegut*

# June 22

20__ __ - _____

_____

20__ __ - _____

_____

20__ __ - _____

_____

20__ __ - _____

_____

20__ __ - _____

_____

## June 23

20___ ___ - _____

_____

20___ ___ - _____

_____

20___ ___ - _____

_____

20___ ___ - _____

_____

20___ ___ - _____

_____

"Live your life that the fear of death

## June 24

20___ ___ - _____

_____

20___ ___ - _____

_____

20___ ___ - _____

_____

20___ ___ - _____

_____

20___ ___ - _____

_____

# June 25

20__ __ - _____

_____

20__ __ - _____

_____

20__ __ - _____

_____

20__ __ - _____

_____

20__ __ - _____

_____

*...can never enter your heart."*
Tecumseh

# June 26

20__ __ - _____

_____

20__ __ - _____

_____

20__ __ - _____

_____

20__ __ - _____

_____

## June 27

20__ __ - _____

_____

20__ __ - _____

_____

20__ __ - _____

_____

20__ __ - _____

_____

20__ __ - _____

_____

"A people that values its privileges above its principles,

## June 28

20__ __ - _____

_____

20__ __ - _____

_____

20__ __ - _____

_____

20__ __ - _____

_____

20__ __ - _____

_____

# June 29

20__ __ - _____

_____

20__ __ - _____

_____

20__ __ - _____

_____

20__ __ - _____

_____

20__ __ - _____

_____

*...soon loses both."*
Dwight D. Eisenhower

# June 30

20__ __ - _____

_____

20__ __ - _____

_____

20__ __ - _____

_____

20__ __ - _____

_____

20__ __ - _____

_____

# June Month End Summary

20__ __ - _____
_____
_____

20__ __ - _____
_____
_____

20__ __ - _____
_____
_____

20__ __ - _____
_____
_____

20__ __ - _____
_____
_____

"Aim for the moon. If you miss, you may hit a star."
W. Clement Stone

# Year 1 – Second Quarter Highlights
## April thru June 20 __ __

## What Was My Favorite...

Adventure_____

Book I Read _____

Day _____

Dream_____

Event_____

Exercise_____

Experience_____

Family Moment_____

Gift Given_____

Gift Received_____

Idea_____

Lesson_____

Meal_____

Movie_____

Person_____

Quote_____

Reflection_____

Relaxation_____

Song_____

Spiritual Moment_____

Success_____

Thought_____

TV Show_____

Volunteering_____

Wish _____

Other _____

Other _____

Other _____

## Year 2 – Second Quarter Highlights
## April thru June 20 ___ ___

## What Was My Favorite...

Adventure_____

Book I Read _____

Day _____

Dream_____

Event_____

Exercise_____

Experience_____

Family Moment_____

Gift Given_____

Gift Received_____

Idea_____

Lesson_____

Meal_____

Movie_____

Person_____

Quote_____

Reflection_____

Relaxation_____

Song_____

Spiritual Moment_____

Success_____

Thought_____

TV Show_____

Volunteering_____

Wish _____

Other _____

Other _____

Other _____

## Year 3 – Second Quarter Highlights
## April thru June 20 __ __

## What Was My Favorite…

Adventure_____

Book I Read _____

Day _____

Dream_____

Event_____

Exercise_____

Experience_____

Family Moment_____

Gift Given_____

Gift Received_____

Idea_____

Lesson_____

Meal_____

Movie_____

Person_____

Quote_____

Reflection_____

Relaxation_____

Song_____

Spiritual Moment_____

Success_____

Thought_____

TV Show_____

Volunteering_____

Wish _____

Other _____

Other _____

Other _____

## Year 4 – Second Quarter Highlights
## April thru June 20 ___ ___

## What Was My Favorite...

Adventure_____

Book I Read _____

Day _____

Dream_____

Event_____

Exercise_____

Experience_____

Family Moment_____

Gift Given_____

Gift Received_____

Idea_____

Lesson_____

Meal_____

Movie_____

Person_____

Quote_____

Reflection_____

Relaxation_____

Song_____

Spiritual Moment_____

Success_____

Thought_____

TV Show_____

Volunteering_____

Wish _____

Other _____

Other _____

Other _____

## Year 5 – Second Quarter Highlights
## April through June 20 __ __

## What Was My Favorite...

Adventure_____

Book I Read _____

Day _____

Dream_____

Event_____

Exercise_____

Experience_____

Family Moment_____

Gift Given_____

Gift Received_____

Idea_____

Lesson_____

Meal_____

Movie_____

Person_____

Quote_____

Reflection_____

Relaxation_____

Song_____

Spiritual Moment_____

Success_____

Thought_____

TV Show_____

Volunteering_____

Wish _____

Other _____

Other _____

Other _____

# July Focus Thought

*Before beginning this month of your journal, on the lines provided for each year, summarize where you are and what you are feeling right then, that day. Keep it simple – one word, a few words, or a few short sentences.*

"I do have the confirmed belief that each of life's moments holds a purpose and a gift. There are no accidents. Nothing is random. Life's lessons come hand-in-hand with their opportunities. Life's lessons are the experiences that come to me to learn more about myself – to learn more about the world that surrounds me."

Doreene Clement

20__ __ - _____

_____

20__ __ - _____

_____

20__ __ - _____

_____

20__ __ - _____

_____

20__ __ - _____

_____

# July 1

20__ __ - _____

_____

20__ __ - _____

_____

20__ __ - _____

_____

20__ __ - _____

_____

20__ __ - _____

_____

*"People buy into the leader before they buy into the vision."*
John Maxwell

# July 2

20__ __ - _____

_____

20__ __ - _____

_____

20__ __ - _____

_____

20__ __ - _____

_____

20__ __ - _____

_____

## July 3

20__ __ - _____

_____

20__ __ - _____

_____

20__ __ - _____

_____

20__ __ - _____

_____

20__ __ - _____

_____

*"As we look into the next century,*

## July 4

20__ __ - _____

_____

20__ __ - _____

_____

20__ __ - _____

_____

20__ __ - _____

_____

20__ __ - _____

_____

# July 5

20__ __ - _____

_____

_____

20__ __ - _____

_____

_____

20__ __ - _____

_____

_____

20__ __ - _____

_____

_____

20__ __ - _____

_____

_____

...leaders will be those who empower others."
Bill Gates

# July 6

20__ __ - _____

_____

_____

20__ __ - _____

_____

_____

20__ __ - _____

_____

_____

20__ __ - _____

_____

_____

20__ __ - _____

_____

_____

## July 7

20___ ___ - _____

_____

20___ ___ - _____

_____

20___ ___ - _____

_____

20___ ___ - _____

_____

20___ ___ - _____

_____

"If a person is unhappy with any aspect of his life

## July 8

20___ ___ - _____

_____

20___ ___ - _____

_____

20___ ___ - _____

_____

20___ ___ - _____

_____

20___ ___ - _____

_____

# July 9

20__ __ - _____

_____

20__ __ - _____

_____

20__ __ - _____

_____

20__ __ - _____

_____

20__ __ - _____

_____

…time, effort, and persistence can change things."
Andrea Samadi

# July 10

20__ __ - _____

_____

20__ __ - _____

_____

20__ __ - _____

_____

20__ __ - _____

_____

20__ __ - _____

_____

## July 11

20__ __ - _____

_____

20__ __ - _____

_____

20__ __ - _____

_____

20__ __ - _____

_____

20__ __ - _____

_____

"Ask, 'What would be loving myself?' The world only wins when

## July 12

20__ __ - _____

_____

20__ __ - _____

_____

20__ __ - _____

_____

20__ __ - _____

_____

20__ __ - _____

_____

## July 13

20____ __ - _____

_____

20____ __ - _____

_____

20____ __ - _____

_____

20____ __ - _____

_____

20____ __ - _____

_____

...I act according to what I hear when I answer this question."
Catherine 'Coky' Gray

## July 14

20____ __ - _____

_____

20____ __ - _____

_____

20____ __ - _____

_____

20____ __ - _____

_____

20____ __ - _____

_____

## July 15

20__ __ - _____

_____

20__ __ - _____

_____

20__ __ - _____

_____

20__ __ - _____

_____

20__ __ - _____

_____

"In order to succeed, your desire for success

## July 16

20__ __ - _____

_____

20__ __ - _____

_____

20__ __ - _____

_____

20__ __ - _____

_____

20__ __ - _____

_____

## July 17

20__ __ - _____

_____

_____

20__ __ - _____

_____

_____

20__ __ - _____

_____

_____

20__ __ - _____

_____

_____

20__ __ - _____

_____

_____

*...should be greater than your fear of failure."*
Bill Cosby

## July 18

20__ __ - _____

_____

_____

20__ __ - _____

_____

_____

20__ __ - _____

_____

_____

20__ __ - _____

_____

_____

20__ __ - _____

_____

_____

## July 19

20__ __ - _____

_____

20__ __ - _____

_____

20__ __ - _____

_____

20__ __ - _____

_____

20__ __ - _____

_____

"It is necessary to the happiness of man

## July 20

20__ __ - _____

_____

20__ __ - _____

_____

20__ __ - _____

_____

20__ __ - _____

_____

20__ __ - _____

_____

# July 21

20__ __ - _____

_____

20__ __ - _____

_____

20__ __ - _____

_____

20__ __ - _____

_____

20__ __ - _____

_____

*...that he be mentally faithful to himself."*
Thomas Paine

# July 22

20__ __ - _____

_____

20__ __ - _____

_____

20__ __ - _____

_____

20__ __ - _____

_____

20__ __ - _____

_____

# July 23

20__ __ - _____

_____

_____

20__ __ - _____

_____

_____

20__ __ - _____

_____

_____

20__ __ - _____

_____

_____

20__ __ - _____

_____

_____

"Doubt is a pain too lonely to know

# July 24

20__ __ - _____

_____

_____

20__ __ - _____

_____

_____

20__ __ - _____

_____

_____

20__ __ - _____

_____

_____

20__ __ - _____

_____

_____

## July 25

20__ __ - _____

_____

20__ __ - _____

_____

20__ __ - _____

_____

20__ __ - _____

_____

20__ __ - _____

_____

*…that faith is his twin brother."*
Kahil Gibran

## July 26

20__ __ - _____

_____

20__ __ - _____

_____

20__ __ - _____

_____

20__ __ - _____

_____

20__ __ - _____

_____

## July 27

20__ __ - _____

_____

20__ __ - _____

_____

20__ __ - _____

_____

20__ __ - _____

_____

20__ __ - _____

_____

"All action results from thought,

## July 28

20__ __ - _____

_____

20__ __ - _____

_____

20__ __ - _____

_____

20__ __ - _____

_____

20__ __ - _____

_____

# July 29

20__ __ - _____

_____

20__ __ - _____

_____

20__ __ - _____

_____

20__ __ - _____

_____

20__ __ - _____

_____

*...so it is thoughts that matter."*
Sai Baba

# July 30

20__ __ - _____

_____

20__ __ - _____

_____

20__ __ - _____

_____

20__ __ - _____

_____

20__ __ - _____

_____

# July 31

20__ __ - _____

_____

20__ __ - _____

_____

20__ __ - _____

_____

20__ __ - _____

_____

20__ __ - _____

_____

*"I have a room all to myself, it is nature."*
Henry David Thoreau

# July Month End Summary

20__ __ - _____

_____

20__ __ - _____

_____

20__ __ - _____

_____

20__ __ - _____

_____

20__ __ - _____

_____

# Notes, Thoughts, Doodles, Ideas

# August Focus Thought

*Before beginning this month of your journal, on the lines provided for each year, summarize where you are and what you are feeling right then, that day. Keep it simple – one word, a few words, or a few short sentences.*

"We all have dreams and desires. Our own personal wishes and wants.

What if you could just have what you wanted and wished for?

What would that look like, feel like?"

Doreene Clement

20__ __ - _____
_____
_____

20__ __ - _____
_____
_____

20__ __ - _____
_____
_____

20__ __ - _____
_____
_____

20__ __ - _____
_____
_____

# August 1

20__ __ - _____

_____

_____

20__ __ - _____

_____

_____

20__ __ - _____

_____

_____

20__ __ - _____

_____

_____

20__ __ - _____

_____

_____

*"When you cease to dream, you cease to live."*
Malcolm Forbes

# August 2

20__ __ - _____

_____

_____

20__ __ - _____

_____

_____

20__ __ - _____

_____

_____

20__ __ - _____

_____

_____

20__ __ - _____

_____

_____

## August 3

20__ __ - _____

_____

20__ __ - _____

_____

20__ __ - _____

_____

20__ __ - _____

_____

20__ __ - _____

_____

*In times like these, it helps to recall*

## August 4

20__ __ - _____

_____

20__ __ - _____

_____

20__ __ - _____

_____

20__ __ - _____

_____

20__ __ - _____

_____

## August 5

20__ __ - _____

_____

20__ __ - _____

_____

20__ __ - _____

_____

20__ __ - _____

_____

20__ __ - _____

_____

*...that there have always been times like these."*
Paul Harvey

## August 6

20__ __ - _____

_____

20__ __ - _____

_____

20__ __ - _____

_____

20__ __ - _____

_____

20__ __ - _____

_____

## August 7

20____ __ - _____

_____

20____ __ - _____

_____

20____ __ - _____

_____

20____ __ - _____

_____

20____ __ - _____

_____

*"Great minds have purposes,*

## August 8

20____ __ - _____

_____

20____ __ - _____

_____

20____ __ - _____

_____

20____ __ - _____

_____

20____ __ - _____

_____

## August 9

20__ __ - _____

_____

_____

20__ __ - _____

_____

_____

20__ __ - _____

_____

_____

20__ __ - _____

_____

_____

20__ __ - _____

_____

_____

…others have wishes."
Washington Irving

## August 10

20__ __ - _____

_____

_____

20__ __ - _____

_____

_____

20__ __ - _____

_____

_____

20__ __ - _____

_____

_____

20__ __ - _____

_____

_____

## August 11

20__ __ - _____

_____

20__ __ - _____

_____

20__ __ - _____

_____

20__ __ - _____

_____

20__ __ - _____

_____

_____

*"You can't try to do things;*

## August 12

20__ __ - _____

_____

20__ __ - _____

_____

20__ __ - _____

_____

20__ __ - _____

_____

20__ __ - _____

_____

## August 13

20__ __ - _____
_____
_____

20__ __ - _____
_____
_____

20__ __ - _____
_____
_____

20__ __ - _____
_____
_____

20__ __ - _____
_____
_____

*…you simply must do them."*
Ray Bradbury

## August 14

20__ __ - _____
_____
_____

20__ __ - _____
_____
_____

20__ __ - _____
_____
_____

20__ __ - _____
_____
_____

20__ __ - _____
_____
_____

## August 15

20__ __ - _____

_____

_____

20__ __ - _____

_____

_____

20__ __ - _____

_____

_____

20__ __ - _____

_____

_____

20__ __ - _____

_____

_____

"A man of knowledge lives by acting,

## August 16

20__ __ - _____

_____

_____

20__ __ - _____

_____

_____

20__ __ - _____

_____

_____

20__ __ - _____

_____

_____

20__ __ - _____

_____

_____

# August 17

20___ ___ - _____

_____

_____

20___ ___ - _____

_____

_____

20___ ___ - _____

_____

_____

20___ ___ - _____

_____

_____

20___ ___ - _____

_____

_____

*…not by thinking about acting."*
*Carlos Castaneda*

# August 18

20___ ___ - _____

_____

_____

20___ ___ - _____

_____

_____

20___ ___ - _____

_____

_____

20___ ___ - _____

_____

_____

20___ ___ - _____

_____

_____

## August 19

20\_\_ \_\_ - _____

_____

20\_\_ \_\_ - _____

_____

20\_\_ \_\_ - _____

_____

20\_\_ \_\_ - _____

_____

20\_\_ \_\_ - _____

_____

"Don't quit. Suffer now and live the

## August 20

20\_\_ \_\_ - _____

_____

20\_\_ \_\_ - _____

_____

20\_\_ \_\_ - _____

_____

20\_\_ \_\_ - _____

_____

20\_\_ \_\_ - _____

_____

## August 21

20___ ___ - _____

_____

20___ ___ - _____

_____

20___ ___ - _____

_____

20___ ___ - _____

_____

20___ ___ - _____

_____

*...rest of your life as a champion."*
Muhammad Ali

## August 22

20___ ___ - _____

_____

20___ ___ - _____

_____

20___ ___ - _____

_____

20___ ___ - _____

_____

20___ ___ - _____

_____

## August 23

20___ ___ - _____

_____

20___ ___ - _____

_____

20___ ___ - _____

_____

20___ ___ - _____

_____

20___ ___ - _____

_____

*"Noble souls, through dust and heat,*

## August 24

20___ ___ - _____

_____

20___ ___ - _____

_____

20___ ___ - _____

_____

20___ ___ - _____

_____

20___ ___ - _____

_____

## August 25

20__ __ - _____

_____

_____

20__ __ - _____

_____

_____

20__ __ - _____

_____

_____

20__ __ - _____

_____

_____

20__ __ - _____

_____

_____

*...rise from disaster and defeat – the stronger."*
*Henry Wadsworth Longfellow*

## August 26

20__ __ - _____

_____

_____

20__ __ - _____

_____

_____

20__ __ - _____

_____

_____

20__ __ - _____

_____

_____

20__ __ - _____

_____

_____

## August 27

20__ __ - _____

_____

_____

20__ __ - _____

_____

_____

20__ __ - _____

_____

_____

20__ __ - _____

_____

_____

20__ __ - _____

_____

_____

"We are only undefeated

## August 28

20__ __ - _____

_____

_____

20__ __ - _____

_____

_____

20__ __ - _____

_____

_____

20__ __ - _____

_____

_____

20__ __ - _____

_____

_____

# August 29

20__ __ - _____

_____

20__ __ - _____

_____

20__ __ - _____

_____

20__ __ - _____

_____

20__ __ - _____

_____

*...because we have gone on trying."*
T. S. Eliot

# August 30

20__ __ - _____

_____

20__ __ - _____

_____

20__ __ - _____

_____

20__ __ - _____

_____

20__ __ - _____

_____

# August 31

20__ __ - _____

_____

_____

20__ __ - _____

_____

_____

20__ __ - _____

_____

_____

20__ __ - _____

_____

_____

20__ __ - _____

_____

_____

*"It is not the length of life, but the depth of life."*
Ralph Waldo Emerson

# August Month End Summary

20__ __ - _____

_____

_____

20__ __ - _____

_____

_____

20__ __ - _____

_____

_____

20__ __ - _____

_____

_____

20__ __ - _____

_____

_____

# Notes, Thoughts, Doodles, Ideas

# September Focus Thought

*Before beginning this month of your journal, on the lines provided for each year, summarize where you are and what you are feeling right then, that day. Keep it simple – one word, a few words, or a few short sentences.*

"I'm learning about trust, faith, hope, and belief. I don't know the difference of the meaning of each word, or if there even is a difference. This is my leap of faith. Or is it trust? I'm still learning."

Doreene Clement

20__ __ - _____
_____

20__ __ - _____
_____

20__ __ - _____
_____

20__ __ - _____
_____

20__ __ - _____
_____

# September 1

20___ ___ - _____

_____

20___ ___ - _____

_____

20___ ___ - _____

_____

20___ ___ - _____

_____

20___ ___ - _____

_____

*"An essential aspect of creativity is not being afraid to fail."*
Edwin Land

# September 2

20___ ___ - _____

_____

20___ ___ - _____

_____

20___ ___ - _____

_____

20___ ___ - _____

_____

20___ ___ - _____

_____

## September 3

20__ __ - _____

_____

20__ __ - _____

_____

20__ __ - _____

_____

20__ __ - _____

_____

20__ __ - _____

_____

"When you love someone

## September 4

20__ __ - _____

_____

20__ __ - _____

_____

20__ __ - _____

_____

20__ __ - _____

_____

20__ __ - _____

_____

## September 5

20__ __ - _____

_____

_____

20__ __ - _____

_____

_____

20__ __ - _____

_____

_____

20__ __ - _____

_____

_____

20__ __ - _____

_____

_____

*...all of your saved up wishes start coming out."*
Elizabeth Bowen

## September 6

20__ __ - _____

_____

_____

20__ __ - _____

_____

_____

20__ __ - _____

_____

_____

20__ __ - _____

_____

_____

20__ __ - _____

_____

_____

## September 7

20__ __ - _____

_____

20__ __ - _____

_____

20__ __ - _____

_____

20__ __ - _____

_____

20__ __ - _____

_____

"Without change, something sleeps inside us,

## September 8

20__ __ - _____

_____

20__ __ - _____

_____

20__ __ - _____

_____

20__ __ - _____

_____

20__ __ - _____

_____

## September 9

20__ __ - _____

_____

_____

20__ __ - _____

_____

_____

20__ __ - _____

_____

_____

20__ __ - _____

_____

_____

20__ __ - _____

_____

_____

*"…and seldom awakens. The sleeper must awaken."*
Frank Herbert

## September 10

20__ __ - _____

_____

20__ __ - _____

_____

20__ __ - _____

_____

20__ __ - _____

_____

20__ __ - _____

_____

_____

## September 11

20__ __ - _____

_____

20__ __ - _____

_____

20__ __ - _____

_____

20__ __ - _____

_____

20__ __ - _____

_____

"Our deeds still travel with us from afar;

## September 12

20__ __ - _____

_____

20__ __ - _____

_____

20__ __ - _____

_____

20__ __ - _____

_____

20__ __ - _____

_____

# September 13

20__ __ - _____

_____

_____

20__ __ - _____

_____

_____

20__ __ - _____

_____

_____

20__ __ - _____

_____

_____

20__ __ - _____

_____

_____

…and what we have been makes us what we are."
George Eliot aka Mary Ann Evans

# September 14

20__ __ - _____

_____

_____

20__ __ - _____

_____

_____

20__ __ - _____

_____

_____

20__ __ - _____

_____

_____

20__ __ - _____

_____

_____

## September 15

20__ __ - _____

_____

20__ __ - _____

_____

20__ __ - _____

_____

20__ __ - _____

_____

20__ __ - _____

_____

"There is no surprise more magical than the surprise of

## September 16

20__ __ - _____

_____

20__ __ - _____

_____

20__ __ - _____

_____

20__ __ - _____

_____

20__ __ - _____

_____

# September 17

20__ __ - _____

_____

20__ __ - _____

_____

20__ __ - _____

_____

20__ __ - _____

_____

20__ __ - _____

_____

...being loved: It is God's finger on man's shoulder."
Charles Morgan

# September 18

20__ __ - _____

_____

20__ __ - _____

_____

20__ __ - _____

_____

20__ __ - _____

_____

20__ __ - _____

_____

## September 19

20__ __ - _____

_____

_____

20__ __ - _____

_____

_____

20__ __ - _____

_____

_____

20__ __ - _____

_____

_____

20__ __ - _____

_____

_____

*"Nothing is miserable unless you think it so."*
Boethius

## September 20

20__ __ - _____

_____

_____

20__ __ - _____

_____

_____

20__ __ - _____

_____

_____

20__ __ - _____

_____

_____

20__ __ - _____

_____

_____

## September 21

20__ __ - _____

_____

20__ __ - _____

_____

20__ __ - _____

_____

20__ __ - _____

_____

20__ __ - _____

_____

*"Never let the fear of striking out get in your way."*
Babe Ruth

## September 22

20__ __ - _____

_____

20__ __ - _____

_____

20__ __ - _____

_____

20__ __ - _____

_____

20__ __ - _____

_____

## September 23

20__ __ - _____

_____

20__ __ - _____

_____

20__ __ - _____

_____

20__ __ - _____

_____

20__ __ - _____

_____

*"My faith is brightest*

## September 24

20__ __ - _____

_____

20__ __ - _____

_____

20__ __ - _____

_____

20__ __ - _____

_____

20__ __ - _____

_____

## September 25

20__ __ - _____

_____

_____

20__ __ - _____

_____

_____

20__ __ - _____

_____

_____

20__ __ - _____

_____

_____

20__ __ - _____

_____

_____

*...in the midst of impenetrable darkness."*
*Mahatma Gandhi*

## September 26

20__ __ - _____

_____

_____

20__ __ - _____

_____

_____

20__ __ - _____

_____

_____

20__ __ - _____

_____

_____

20__ __ - _____

_____

_____

## September 27

20__ __ - _____

_____

20__ __ - _____

_____

20__ __ - _____

_____

20__ __ - _____

_____

20__ __ - _____

_____

*"They always say time changes things,*

## September 28

20__ __ - _____

_____

20__ __ - _____

_____

20__ __ - _____

_____

20__ __ - _____

_____

20__ __ - _____

_____

# September 29

20__ __ - _____

_____

_____

20__ __ - _____

_____

_____

20__ __ - _____

_____

_____

20__ __ - _____

_____

_____

20__ __ - _____

_____

_____

*...but you actually have to change them yourself."*
*Andy Warhol*

# September 30

20__ __ - _____

_____

_____

20__ __ - _____

_____

_____

20__ __ - _____

_____

_____

20__ __ - _____

_____

_____

20__ __ - _____

_____

_____

# September Month End Summary

20__ __ - _____
_____
_____

20__ __ - _____
_____
_____

20__ __ - _____
_____
_____

20__ __ - _____
_____
_____

20__ __ - _____
_____
_____

"If you can dream it, you can do it."
Walt Disney

# Year 1 – Third Quarter Highlights
## July through September 20 __ __

## What Was My Favorite...

Adventure_____

Book I Read _____

Day _____

Dream_____

Event_____

Exercise_____

Experience_____

Family Moment_____

Gift Given_____

Gift Received_____

Idea_____

Lesson_____

Meal_____

Movie_____

Person_____

Quote_____

Reflection_____

Relaxation_____

Song_____

Spiritual Moment_____

Success_____

Thought_____

TV Show_____

Volunteering_____

Wish _____

Other _____

Other _____

Other _____

## Year 2 – Third Quarter Highlights
## July through September 20 __ __

## What Was My Favorite...

Adventure_____

Book I Read _____

Day _____

Dream_____

Event_____

Exercise_____

Experience_____

Family Moment_____

Gift Given_____

Gift Received_____

Idea_____

Lesson_____

Meal_____

Movie_____

Person_____

Quote_____

Reflection_____

Relaxation_____

Song_____

Spiritual Moment_____

Success_____

Thought_____

TV Show_____

Volunteering_____

Wish _____

Other _____

Other _____

Other _____

## Year 3 – Third Quarter Highlights
## July through September 20 __ __

## What Was My Favorite...

Adventure_____

Book I Read _____

Day _____

Dream_____

Event_____

Exercise_____

Experience_____

Family Moment_____

Gift Given_____

Gift Received_____

Idea_____

Lesson_____

Meal_____

Movie_____

Person_____

Quote_____

Reflection_____

Relaxation_____

Song_____

Spiritual Moment_____

Success_____

Thought_____

TV Show_____

Volunteering_____

Wish _____

Other _____

Other _____

Other _____

## Year 4 – Third Quarter Highlights
## July through September 20 __ __

## What Was My Favorite...

Adventure_____

Book I Read _____

Day _____

Dream_____

Event_____

Exercise_____

Experience_____

Family Moment_____

Gift Given_____

Gift Received_____

Idea_____

Lesson_____

Meal_____

Movie_____

Person_____

Quote_____

Reflection_____

Relaxation_____

Song_____

Spiritual Moment_____

Success_____

Thought_____

TV Show_____

Volunteering_____

Wish _____

Other _____

Other _____

Other _____

## Year 5 - Third Quarter Highlights
## July through September 20 __ __

## What Was My Favorite...

Adventure_____

Book I Read _____

Day _____

Dream_____

Event_____

Exercise_____

Experience_____

Family Moment_____

Gift Given_____

Gift Received_____

Idea_____

Lesson_____

Meal_____

Movie_____

Person_____

Quote_____

Reflection_____

Relaxation_____

Song_____

Spiritual Moment_____

Success_____

Thought_____

TV Show_____

Volunteering_____

Wish _____

Other _____

Other _____

Other _____

# October Focus Thought

*Before beginning this month of your journal, on the lines provided for each year, summarize where you are and what you are feeling right then, that day. Keep it simple – one word, a few words, or a few short sentences.*

"There's nothing like putting pen to paper to instill you with a sense of optimism, anticipation and excitement about your goals or aspirations."

Doreene Clement

20__ __ - _____
_____
_____

20__ __ - _____
_____
_____

20__ __ - _____
_____
_____

20__ __ - _____
_____
_____

20__ __ - _____
_____
_____

# October 1

20__ __ - _____
_____
_____

20__ __ - _____
_____
_____

20__ __ - _____
_____
_____

20__ __ - _____
_____
_____

20__ __ - _____
_____
_____

*"The best way to predict your future is to create it."*
Abraham Lincoln

# October 2

20__ __ - _____
_____
_____

20__ __ - _____
_____
_____

20__ __ - _____
_____
_____

20__ __ - _____
_____
_____

20__ __ - _____
_____
_____

## October 3

20__ __ - _____

_____

_____

20__ __ - _____

_____

_____

20__ __ - _____

_____

_____

20__ __ - _____

_____

_____

20__ __ - _____

_____

_____

*"Be faithful in small things,*

## October 4

20__ __ - _____

_____

_____

20__ __ - _____

_____

_____

20__ __ - _____

_____

_____

20__ __ - _____

_____

_____

20__ __ - _____

_____

_____

## October 5

20___ ___ - _____

_____

20___ ___ - _____

_____

20___ ___ - _____

_____

20___ ___ - _____

_____

20___ ___ - _____

_____

*...because it is in them that your strength lies."*
*Mother Teresa*

## October 6

20___ ___ - _____

_____

20___ ___ - _____

_____

20___ ___ - _____

_____

20___ ___ - _____

_____

20___ ___ - _____

_____

## October 7

20__ __ - _____

_____

20__ __ - _____

_____

20__ __ - _____

_____

20__ __ - _____

_____

20__ __ - _____

_____

*"An honest heart being the first blessing,*

## October 8

20__ __ - _____

_____

20__ __ - _____

_____

20__ __ - _____

_____

20__ __ - _____

_____

20__ __ - _____

_____

# October 9

20___ ___ - _____

_____

_____

20___ ___ - _____

_____

_____

20___ ___ - _____

_____

_____

20___ ___ - _____

_____

_____

20___ ___ - _____

_____

_____

...a knowing head is the second."
Thomas Jefferson

# October 10

20___ ___ - _____

_____

_____

20___ ___ - _____

_____

_____

20___ ___ - _____

_____

_____

20___ ___ - _____

_____

_____

20___ ___ - _____

_____

_____

## October 11

20___ ___ - _____

_____

20___ ___ - _____

_____

20___ ___ - _____

_____

20___ ___ - _____

_____

20___ ___ - _____

_____

"Stubborn and ardent clinging to one's opinion

## October 12

20___ ___ - _____

_____

20___ ___ - _____

_____

20___ ___ - _____

_____

20___ ___ - _____

_____

20___ ___ - _____

_____

# October 13

20__ __ - _____

_____

_____

20__ __ - _____

_____

_____

20__ __ - _____

_____

_____

20__ __ - _____

_____

_____

20__ __ - _____

_____

_____

...is the best proof of stupidity."
Michel de Montaigne

# October 14

20__ __ - _____

_____

_____

20__ __ - _____

_____

_____

20__ __ - _____

_____

_____

20__ __ - _____

_____

_____

20__ __ - _____

_____

_____

## October 15

20___ ___ - _____

_____

20___ ___ - _____

_____

20___ ___ - _____

_____

20___ ___ - _____

_____

20___ ___ - _____

_____

*"Happiness often sneaks in through a*

## October 16

20___ ___ - _____

_____

20___ ___ - _____

_____

20___ ___ - _____

_____

20___ ___ - _____

_____

20___ ___ - _____

_____

# October 17

20__ __ - _____

_____

_____

20__ __ - _____

_____

_____

20__ __ - _____

_____

_____

20__ __ - _____

_____

_____

20__ __ - _____

_____

_____

*…you didn't know you left open."*
John Barrymore

# October 18

20__ __ - _____

_____

_____

20__ __ - _____

_____

_____

20__ __ - _____

_____

_____

20__ __ - _____

_____

_____

20__ __ - _____

_____

_____

## October 19

20__ __ - _____

_____

20__ __ - _____

_____

20__ __ - _____

_____

20__ __ - _____

_____

20__ __ - _____

_____

"Fame is a vapor, popularity an accident, and riches take wings.

## October 20

20__ __ - _____

_____

20__ __ - _____

_____

20__ __ - _____

_____

20__ __ - _____

_____

20__ __ - _____

_____

# October 21

20__ __ - _____

_____

_____

20__ __ - _____

_____

_____

20__ __ - _____

_____

_____

20__ __ - _____

_____

_____

20__ __ - _____

_____

_____

*...Only one thing endures and that is character."*
Horace Greeley

# October 22

20__ __ - _____

_____

_____

20__ __ - _____

_____

_____

20__ __ - _____

_____

_____

20__ __ - _____

_____

_____

20__ __ - _____

_____

_____

# October 23

20__ __ - _____

_____

20__ __ - _____

_____

20__ __ - _____

_____

20__ __ - _____

_____

20__ __ - _____

_____

"Vitality shows in not only the ability to persist

# October 24

20__ __ - _____

_____

20__ __ - _____

_____

20__ __ - _____

_____

20__ __ - _____

_____

20__ __ - _____

_____

# October 25

20__ __ - _____

_____

20__ __ - _____

_____

20__ __ - _____

_____

20__ __ - _____

_____

20__ __ - _____

_____

...but the ability to start over."
Francis Scott Fitzgerald

# October 26

20__ __ - _____

_____

20__ __ - _____

_____

20__ __ - _____

_____

20__ __ - _____

_____

20__ __ - _____

_____

## October 27

20___ ___ - _____

_____

20___ ___ - _____

_____

20___ ___ - _____

_____

20___ ___ - _____

_____

20___ ___ - _____

_____

*"Four be the things I am wiser to know:*

## October 28

20___ ___ - _____

_____

20___ ___ - _____

_____

20___ ___ - _____

_____

20___ ___ - _____

_____

20___ ___ - _____

_____

# October 29

20___ ___ - _____

_____

_____

20___ ___ - _____

_____

_____

20___ ___ - _____

_____

_____

20___ ___ - _____

_____

_____

20___ ___ - _____

_____

_____

…Idleness, sorrow, a friend, and a foe."
Dorothy Parker

# October 30

20___ ___ - _____

_____

_____

20___ ___ - _____

_____

_____

20___ ___ - _____

_____

_____

20___ ___ - _____

_____

_____

20___ ___ - _____

_____

_____

# October 31

20___ ___ - _____
_____
_____

20___ ___ - _____
_____
_____

20___ ___ - _____
_____
_____

20___ ___ - _____
_____
_____

20___ ___ - _____
_____
_____

*"The art of living is more like wrestling than dancing."*
Marcus Aurelius

# October Month End Summary

20___ ___ - _____
_____
_____

20___ ___ - _____
_____
_____

20___ ___ - _____
_____
_____

20___ ___ - _____
_____
_____

20___ ___ - _____
_____
_____

# Notes, Thoughts, Doodles, Ideas

# November Focus Thought

*Before beginning this month of your journal, on the lines provided for each year, summarize where you are and what you are feeling right then, that day. Keep it simple – one word, a few words, or a few short sentences.*

"Everyone has a story. Your experiences, your feelings, ideas, thoughts, and dreams all combine to form your life and your journey, which is your story."

Doreene Clement

20__ __ - _____

_____

20__ __ - _____

_____

20__ __ - _____

_____

20__ __ - _____

_____

20__ __ - _____

_____

# November 1

20__ __ - _____

_____

_____

20__ __ - _____

_____

_____

20__ __ - _____

_____

_____

20__ __ - _____

_____

_____

20__ __ - _____

_____

_____

*"Smile, it's free therapy."*
Douglas Horton

# November 2

20__ __ - _____

_____

_____

20__ __ - _____

_____

_____

20__ __ - _____

_____

_____

20__ __ - _____

_____

_____

20__ __ - _____

_____

_____

# November 3

20___ ___ - _____

_____

20___ ___ - _____

_____

20___ ___ - _____

_____

20___ ___ - _____

_____

20___ ___ - _____

_____

"Success is not final, failure is not fatal:

# November 4

20___ ___ - _____

_____

20___ ___ - _____

_____

20___ ___ - _____

_____

20___ ___ - _____

_____

20___ ___ - _____

_____

# November 5

20__ __ - _____

_____

_____

20__ __ - _____

_____

_____

20__ __ - _____

_____

_____

20__ __ - _____

_____

_____

20__ __ - _____

_____

_____

*...it is the courage to continue that counts."*
Winston Churchill

# November 6

20__ __ - _____

_____

_____

20__ __ - _____

_____

_____

20__ __ - _____

_____

_____

20__ __ - _____

_____

_____

20__ __ - _____

_____

_____

## November 7

20__ __ - _____

_____

20__ __ - _____

_____

20__ __ - _____

_____

20__ __ - _____

_____

20__ __ - _____

_____

"A man who dares to waste one hour of time

## November 8

20__ __ - _____

_____

20__ __ - _____

_____

20__ __ - _____

_____

20__ __ - _____

_____

20__ __ - _____

_____

# November 9

20__ __ - _____

_____

_____

20__ __ - _____

_____

_____

20__ __ - _____

_____

_____

20__ __ - _____

_____

_____

20__ __ - _____

_____

_____

…has not discovered the value of life."
Charles Darwin

# November 10

20__ __ - _____

_____

_____

20__ __ - _____

_____

_____

20__ __ - _____

_____

_____

20__ __ - _____

_____

_____

20__ __ - _____

_____

_____

# November 11

20__ __ - _____

_____

20__ __ - _____

_____

20__ __ - _____

_____

20__ __ - _____

_____

20__ __ - _____

_____

*"Study the past, if you would divine the future."*
Confucius

# November 12

20__ __ - _____

_____

20__ __ - _____

_____

20__ __ - _____

_____

20__ __ - _____

_____

20__ __ - _____

_____

# November 13

20___ ___ - _____

_____

20___ ___ - _____

_____

20___ ___ - _____

_____

20___ ___ - _____

_____

20___ ___ - _____

_____

*"It is your work in life that is the ultimate seduction."*
Pablo Picasso

# November 14

20___ ___ - _____

_____

20___ ___ - _____

_____

20___ ___ - _____

_____

20___ ___ - _____

_____

20___ ___ - _____

_____

## November 15

20__ __ - _____

_____

_____

20__ __ - _____

_____

_____

20__ __ - _____

_____

_____

20__ __ - _____

_____

_____

20__ __ - _____

_____

_____

*"Don't cry because it's over, smile because it happened."*
Dr. Seuss (Theodor Seuss Geisel)

## November 16

20__ __ - _____

_____

_____

20__ __ - _____

_____

_____

20__ __ - _____

_____

_____

20__ __ - _____

_____

_____

20__ __ - _____

_____

_____

## November 17

20__ __ - _____

_____

_____

20__ __ - _____

_____

_____

20__ __ - _____

_____

_____

20__ __ - _____

_____

_____

20__ __ - _____

_____

_____

*"The future starts today – not tomorrow."*
Pope John Paul II

## November 18

20__ __ - _____

_____

_____

20__ __ - _____

_____

_____

20__ __ - _____

_____

_____

20__ __ - _____

_____

_____

20__ __ - _____

_____

_____

# November 19

20__ __ - _____
_____
_____

20__ __ - _____
_____
_____

20__ __ - _____
_____
_____

20__ __ - _____
_____
_____

20__ __ - _____
_____
_____

*"If you think you can do a thing,"*
Leonardo da Vinci

# November 20

20__ __ - _____
_____
_____

20__ __ - _____
_____
_____

20__ __ - _____
_____

20__ __ - _____
_____

20__ __ - _____
_____
_____

# November 21

20__ __ - _____

_____

_____

20__ __ - _____

_____

_____

20__ __ - _____

_____

_____

20__ __ - _____

_____

_____

20__ __ - _____

_____

_____

*...or think you can't do a thing, you are right."*
*Henry Ford*

# November 22

20__ __ - _____

_____

_____

20__ __ - _____

_____

_____

20__ __ - _____

_____

_____

20__ __ - _____

_____

_____

20__ __ - _____

_____

_____

# November 23

20__ __ - _____

_____

20__ __ - _____

_____

20__ __ - _____

_____

20__ __ - _____

_____

20__ __ - _____

_____

*"There is nothing so powerful as truth,*

# November 24

20__ __ - _____

_____

20__ __ - _____

_____

20__ __ - _____

_____

20__ __ - _____

_____

20__ __ - _____

_____

## November 25

20__ __ - _____

_____

20__ __ - _____

_____

20__ __ - _____

_____

20__ __ - _____

_____

20__ __ - _____

_____

*…and often nothing so strange."*
Daniel Webster

## November 26

20__ __ - _____

_____

20__ __ - _____

_____

20__ __ - _____

_____

20__ __ - _____

_____

20__ __ - _____

_____

## November 27

20__ __ - _____

_____

20__ __ - _____

_____

20__ __ - _____

_____

20__ __ - _____

_____

20__ __ - _____

_____

*"Very often it happens that a discovery is made*

## November 28

20__ __ - _____

_____

20__ __ - _____

_____

20__ __ - _____

_____

20__ __ - _____

_____

20__ __ - _____

_____

## November 29

20__ __ - _____

_____

_____

20__ __ - _____

_____

_____

20__ __ - _____

_____

_____

20__ __ - _____

_____

_____

20__ __ - _____

_____

_____

*…whilst working upon quite another problem."*
Thomas Alva Edison

## November 30

20__ __ - _____

_____

20__ __ - _____

_____

20__ __ - _____

_____

20__ __ - _____

_____

20__ __ - _____

_____

# November Month End Summary

20__ __ - _____
_____
_____

20__ __ - _____
_____
_____

20__ __ - _____
_____
_____

20__ __ - _____
_____
_____

20__ __ - _____
_____
_____

*"The difference between the impossible and the possible lies in a person's determination."*
Tommy Lasorda

# Notes, Thoughts, Doodles, Ideas

# December Focus Thought

*Before beginning this month of your journal, on the lines provided for each year, summarize where you are and what you are feeling right then, that day. Keep it simple – one word, a few words, or a few short sentences.*

"Cancer was not in my budget. Here I am. Recently I found that I have cancer.  After the initial shock I set about figuring out what to do next to support me and this new health challenge.  The process is demanding, but my attitude is great, as I will survive. I will be a Cancer Victor."

Doreene Clement

20___ ___ - _____
_____

20___ ___ - _____
_____

20___ ___ - _____
_____

20___ ___ - _____
_____

20___ ___ - _____
_____

## December 1

20__ __ - _____
_____
_____

20__ __ - _____
_____
_____

20__ __ - _____
_____
_____

20__ __ - _____
_____
_____

20__ __ - _____
_____
_____

"Chocolate is a perfect food, as wholesome as it is

## December 2

20__ __ - _____
_____
_____

20__ __ - _____
_____
_____

20__ __ - _____
_____
_____

20__ __ - _____
_____
_____

20__ __ - _____
_____
_____

# December 3

20__ __ - _____

_____

20__ __ - _____

_____

20__ __ - _____

_____

20__ __ - _____

_____

20__ __ - _____

_____

...delicious; a beneficent restorer of exhausted power. It is

# December 4

20__ __ - _____

_____

20__ __ - _____

_____

20__ __ - _____

_____

20__ __ - _____

_____

20__ __ - _____

_____

# December 5

20__ __ - _____

_____

20__ __ - _____

_____

20__ __ - _____

_____

20__ __ - _____

_____

20__ __ - _____

_____

*...the best friend of those engaged in literary pursuits."*
Justus von Liebig

# December 6

20__ __ - _____

_____

20__ __ - _____

_____

20__ __ - _____

_____

20__ __ - _____

_____

20__ __ - _____

_____

# December 7

20___ ___ - _____
_____
_____

20___ ___ - _____
_____
_____

20___ ___ - _____
_____
_____

20___ ___ - _____
_____
_____

20___ ___ - _____
_____
_____

"To love oneself

# December 8

20___ ___ - _____
_____
_____

20___ ___ - _____
_____
_____

20___ ___ - _____
_____
_____

20___ ___ - _____
_____
_____

20___ ___ - _____
_____
_____

# December 9

20__ __ - _____

_____

_____

20__ __ - _____

_____

_____

20__ __ - _____

_____

_____

20__ __ - _____

_____

_____

20__ __ - _____

_____

_____

…is the beginning of a life-long romance."
Oscar Wilde

# December 10

20__ __ - _____

_____

_____

20__ __ - _____

_____

_____

20__ __ - _____

_____

_____

20__ __ - _____

_____

_____

20__ __ - _____

_____

_____

# December 11

20___ ___ - _____

_____

20___ ___ - _____

_____

20___ ___ - _____

_____

20___ ___ - _____

_____

20___ ___ - _____

_____

"Pain is inevitable.

# December 12

20___ ___ - _____

_____

20___ ___ - _____

_____

20___ ___ - _____

_____

20___ ___ - _____

_____

20___ ___ - _____

_____

# December 13

20__ __ - _____

_____

_____

20__ __ - _____

_____

_____

20__ __ - _____

_____

_____

20__ __ - _____

_____

_____

20__ __ - _____

_____

_____

*...Suffering is optional."*
*Haruki Murakami*

# December 14

20__ __ - _____

_____

_____

20__ __ - _____

_____

_____

20__ __ - _____

_____

20__ __ - _____

_____

20__ __ - _____

_____

_____

## December 15

20__ __ - _____

_____

_____

20__ __ - _____

_____

_____

20__ __ - _____

_____

_____

20__ __ - _____

_____

_____

20__ __ - _____

_____

_____

*"Hold fast to dreams, for if dreams die,*

## December 16

20__ __ - _____

_____

_____

20__ __ - _____

_____

_____

20__ __ - _____

_____

_____

20__ __ - _____

_____

_____

20__ __ - _____

_____

_____

# December 17

20__ __ - _____

_____

_____

20__ __ - _____

_____

_____

20__ __ - _____

_____

_____

20__ __ - _____

_____

_____

20__ __ - _____

_____

_____

*…life is a broken-winged bird that cannot fly."*
Langston Hughes

# December 18

20__ __ - _____

_____

_____

20__ __ - _____

_____

_____

20__ __ - _____

_____

_____

20__ __ - _____

_____

_____

20__ __ - _____

_____

_____

# December 19

20___ ___ - _____

_____

20___ ___ - _____

_____

20___ ___ - _____

_____

20___ ___ - _____

_____

20___ ___ - _____

_____

"One man's theology

# December 20

20___ ___ - _____

_____

20___ ___ - _____

_____

20___ ___ - _____

_____

20___ ___ - _____

_____

20___ ___ - _____

_____

# December 21

20____ ___ - _____

_____

_____

20____ ___ - _____

_____

_____

20____ ___ - _____

_____

_____

20____ ___ - _____

_____

_____

20____ ___ - _____

_____

_____

*...is another man's belly laugh."*
*Robert A. Heinlein*

# December 22

20____ ___ - _____

_____

_____

20____ ___ - _____

_____

_____

20____ ___ - _____

_____

_____

20____ ___ - _____

_____

_____

20____ ___ - _____

_____

_____

## December 23

20__ __ - _____

_____

20__ __ - _____

_____

20__ __ - _____

_____

20__ __ - _____

_____

20__ __ - _____

_____

"What the caterpillar calls the end of the world,

## December 24

20__ __ - _____

_____

20__ __ - _____

_____

20__ __ - _____

_____

20__ __ - _____

_____

20__ __ - _____

_____

# December 25

20__ __ - _____

_____

20__ __ - _____

_____

20__ __ - _____

_____

20__ __ - _____

_____

20__ __ - _____

_____

...the Master calls a butterfly."
Richard Bach

# December 26

20__ __ - _____

_____

20__ __ - _____

_____

20__ __ - _____

_____

20__ __ - _____

_____

20__ __ - _____

_____

## December 27

20__ __ - _____

_____

20__ __ - _____

_____

20__ __ - _____

_____

20__ __ - _____

_____

20__ __ - _____

_____

"What I think about, I bring about. The thought of success will

## December 28

20__ __ - _____

_____

20__ __ - _____

_____

20__ __ - _____

_____

20__ __ - _____

_____

20__ __ - _____

_____

# December 29

20__ __ - _____
_____
_____

20__ __ - _____
_____
_____

20__ __ - _____
_____
_____

20__ __ - _____
_____
_____

20__ __ - _____
_____
_____

...foster success. The thought of love will foster love.

# December 30

20__ __ - _____
_____
_____

20__ __ - _____
_____
_____

20__ __ - _____
_____
_____

20__ __ - _____
_____
_____

20__ __ - _____
_____
_____

# December 31

20__ __ - _____

_____

_____

20__ __ - _____

_____

_____

20__ __ - _____

_____

_____

20__ __ - _____

_____

_____

20__ __ - _____

_____

_____

*…What am I thinking about today?"*
*Rita Davenport*

# December Month End Summary

20__ __ - _____

_____

_____

20__ __ - _____

_____

_____

20__ __ - _____

_____

_____

20__ __ - _____

_____

_____

20__ __ - _____

_____

_____

## Year 1 – Fourth Quarter Highlights
## October thru December 20 __ __

## What Was My Favorite...

Adventure_____

Book I Read _____

Day _____

Dream_____

Event_____

Exercise_____

Experience_____

Family Moment_____

Gift Given_____

Gift Received_____

Idea_____

Lesson_____

Meal_____

Movie_____

Person_____

Quote_____

Reflection_____

Relaxation_____

Song_____

Spiritual Moment_____

Success_____

Thought_____

TV Show_____

Volunteering_____

Wish _____

Other _____

Other _____

Other _____

## Year 2 – Fourth Quarter Highlights
## October thru December 20 __ __

## What Was My Favorite...

Adventure_____

Book I Read _____

Day _____

Dream_____

Event_____

Exercise_____

Experience_____

Family Moment_____

Gift Given_____

Gift Received_____

Idea_____

Lesson_____

Meal_____

Movie_____

Person_____

Quote_____

Reflection_____

Relaxation_____

Song_____

Spiritual Moment_____

Success_____

Thought_____

TV Show_____

Volunteering_____

Wish _____

Other _____

Other _____

Other _____

## Year 3 – Fourth Quarter Highlight
## October thru December 20 __ __

## What Was My Favorite...

Adventure_____

Book I Read _____

Day _____

Dream_____

Event_____

Exercise_____

Experience_____

Family Moment_____

Gift Given_____

Gift Received_____

Idea_____

Lesson_____

Meal_____

Movie_____

Person_____

Quote_____

Reflection_____

Relaxation_____

Song_____

Spiritual Moment_____

Success_____

Thought_____

TV Show_____

Volunteering_____

Wish _____

Other _____

Other _____

Other _____

## Year 4 – Fourth Quarter Highlights
## October thru December 20 __ __

## What Was My Favorite...

Adventure_____

Book I Read _____

Day _____

Dream_____

Event_____

Exercise_____

Experience_____

Family Moment_____

Gift Given_____

Gift Received_____

Idea_____

Lesson_____

Meal_____

Movie_____

Person_____

Quote_____

Reflection_____

Relaxation_____

Song_____

Spiritual Moment_____

Success_____

Thought_____

TV Show_____

Volunteering_____

Wish _____

Other _____

Other _____

Other _____

# Year 5 – Fourth Quarter Highlights
## October thru December 20 __ __

## What Was My Favorite...

Adventure_____

Book I Read _____

Day _____

Dream_____

Event_____

Exercise_____

Experience_____

Family Moment_____

Gift Given_____

Gift Received_____

Idea_____

Lesson_____

Meal_____

Movie_____

Person_____

Quote_____

Reflection_____

Relaxation_____

Song_____

Spiritual Moment_____

Success_____

Thought_____

TV Show_____

Volunteering_____

Wish _____

Other _____

Other _____

Other _____

# Notes, Thoughts, Doodles, Ideas

# THE 5 YEAR JOURNAL

## Encouragement to Keep on Journalizing Next Year

The end of this year is here. It is now time to turn the page into the next year, your New Year. A whole new unwritten script awaits you. More thoughts, more feelings, more of life to be experienced and written down. This Journal, these writings, your writings are <u>for</u> you. For your benefit. For your growth.

- Take some time for yourself, with your Journal, at the end of this year or the beginning of the New Year and reflect.
- Find a quiet time. Find a quiet place.
- Re-read your Journal. Browse through or read it cover to cover.
- Evaluate where you are at today; reflect on where you've come from, and think about where you want to go in your life.
- Remember all that you accomplished this last year. Honor it and yourself.
- Realize how you have changed.
- Think about what you still want to change.
- Take an honest look at yourself and all that you are.
- Even look at what you may not be now.
- You now have the tool of your Journal to add to your life and well-being.
- Experience what you've said, what you've felt, what you've wanted, what you got.
- Remember. Reflect.
- Use your Journal to assist you in the experiences of your life, your daily living.
- Set your Goals for the New Year; write them in your Journal.
- Determine your Resolutions; write them down in your Journal.
- Continue your habit of scheduling a place and a time for you and your Journal.
- Daily, keep tracking your life in your Journal.
- Write it down, get it out.
- Your Journal is a tool that can assist you with the work and the fun in life, of life.
- Re-read Doreene's Reflections and Using This Journal & Workbook Sections.

The day will arrive when your Journal is full – 5 years will have passed, and you will be starting another 5 YEAR JOURNAL. You'll have placed your Journal in that special place, proud as you pass by, realizing your accomplishments – what you have gained and what you have given.

# Notes, Thoughts, Doodles, Ideas

# Year One Highlights 20 __ __

## What Was My Favorite...

Adventure_____

Book I Read _____

Day _____

Dream_____

Event_____

Exercise_____

Experience_____

Family Moment_____

Gift Given_____

Gift Received_____

Idea_____

Lesson_____

Meal_____

Movie_____

Person_____

Quote_____

Reflection_____

Relaxation_____

Song_____

Spiritual Moment_____

Success_____

Thought_____

TV Show_____

Volunteering_____

Wish _____

Other _____

Other _____

Other _____

# Year Two Highlights 20 __ __

## What Was My Favorite...

Adventure_____

Book I Read _____

Day _____

Dream_____

Event_____

Exercise_____

Experience_____

Family Moment_____

Gift Given_____

Gift Received_____

Idea_____

Lesson_____

Meal_____

Movie_____

Person_____

Quote_____

Reflection_____

Relaxation_____

Song_____

Spiritual Moment_____

Success_____

Thought_____

TV Show_____

Volunteering_____

Wish _____

Other _____

Other _____

Other _____

# Year Three Highlights 20 __ __

## What Was My Favorite...

Adventure_____

Book I Read _____

Day _____

Dream_____

Event_____

Exercise_____

Experience_____

Family Moment_____

Gift Given_____

Gift Received_____

Idea_____

Lesson_____

Meal_____

Movie_____

Person_____

Quote_____

Reflection_____

Relaxation_____

Song_____

Spiritual Moment_____

Success_____

Thought_____

TV Show_____

Volunteering_____

Wish _____

Other _____

Other _____

Other _____

# Year Four Highlights 20 __ __

## What Was My Favorite...

Adventure_____

Book I Read _____

Day _____

Dream_____

Event_____

Exercise_____

Experience_____

Family Moment_____

Gift Given_____

Gift Received_____

Idea_____

Lesson_____

Meal_____

Movie_____

Person_____

Quote_____

Reflection_____

Relaxation_____

Song_____

Spiritual Moment_____

Success_____

Thought_____

TV Show_____

Volunteering_____

Wish _____

Other _____

Other _____

Other _____

# Year Five Highlights 20 __ __

## What Was My Favorite...

Adventure_____

Book I Read _____

Day _____

Dream_____

Event_____

Exercise_____

Experience_____

Family Moment_____

Gift Given_____

Gift Received_____

Idea_____

Lesson_____

Meal_____

Movie_____

Person_____

Quote_____

Reflection_____

Relaxation_____

Song_____

Spiritual Moment_____

Success_____

Thought_____

TV Show_____

Volunteering_____

Wish _____

Other _____

Other _____

Other _____

# Notes, Thoughts, Doodles, Ideas

# The Best Thing That Happened This Year Was...

20__ __ - _____
_____
_____

20__ __ - _____
_____
_____

20__ __ - _____
_____
_____

20__ __ - _____
_____
_____

20__ __ - _____
_____
_____

# The Worst Thing That Happened This Year Was...

20__ __ - _____
_____
_____

20__ __ - _____
_____
_____

20__ __ - _____
_____
_____

20__ __ - _____
_____
_____

20__ __ - _____
_____
_____

# Q & A Year One  20 __ __

Name three likes –

_____

_____

_____

Name three dislikes –

_____

_____

_____

Name three good/easy things that happened this year –

_____

_____

_____

Name three bad/hard things that happened this year –

_____

_____

_____

What did I do for myself this year?

_____

_____

_____

_____

What did I do that did not support me this year?

_____

_____

_____

_____

# Q & A Year One 20 __ __

If I could change one thing about myself, what would that be?

_____

_____

_____

If I could change one thing about my life, what would that be?

_____

_____

_____

If I could change one thing about the world, what would it be?

_____

_____

_____

What three things have I changed or done differently this year?

_____

_____

_____

What are three things I have kept the same?

_____

_____

_____

What are three things I was reluctant to do, but did them anyway?

_____

_____

_____

What are three things I was reluctant to do, but want to next year?

_____

_____

_____

# Q & A Year Two 20 __ __

Name three likes –
_____
_____
_____

Name three dislikes –
_____
_____
_____

Name three good/easy things that happened this year –
_____
_____
_____

Name three bad/hard things that happened this year –
_____
_____
_____

What did I do for myself this year?
_____
_____
_____
_____

What did I do that did not support me this year?
_____
_____
_____
_____

# Q & A Year Two 20 __ __

If I could change one thing about myself, what would that be?

_____

_____

_____

If I could change one thing about my life, what would that be?

_____

_____

_____

If I could change one thing about the world, what would it be?

_____

_____

_____

What three things have I changed or done differently this year?

_____

_____

_____

What are three things I have kept the same?

_____

_____

_____

What are three things I was reluctant to do, but did them anyway?

_____

_____

_____

What are three things I was reluctant to do, but want to next year?

_____

_____

_____

# Q & A Year Three 20 __ __

Name three likes –

_____

_____

_____

Name three dislikes –

_____

_____

_____

Name three good/easy things that happened this year –

_____

_____

_____

Name three bad/hard things that happened this year –

_____

_____

_____

What did I do for myself this year?

_____

_____

_____

_____

What did I do that did not support me this year?

_____

_____

_____

_____

# Q & A Year Three 20 __ __

If I could change one thing about myself, what would that be?

_____

_____

_____

If I could change one thing about my life, what would that be?

_____

_____

_____

If I could change one thing about the world, what would it be?

_____

_____

_____

What three things have I changed or done differently this year?

_____

_____

_____

What are three things I have kept the same?

_____

_____

_____

What are three things I was reluctant to do, but did them anyway?

_____

_____

_____

What are three things I was reluctant to do, but want to next year?

_____

_____

_____

# Q & A Year Four 20 __ __

Name three likes –

_____
_____
_____

Name three dislikes –

_____
_____
_____

Name three good/easy things that happened this year –

_____
_____
_____

Name three bad/hard things that happened this year –

_____
_____
_____

What did I do for myself this year?

_____
_____
_____
_____

What did I do that did not support me this year?

_____
_____
_____
_____

# Q & A Year Four 20 __ __

If I could change one thing about myself, what would that be?

_____

_____

_____

If I could change one thing about my life, what would that be?

_____

_____

_____

If I could change one thing about the world, what would it be?

_____

_____

_____

What three things have I changed or done differently this year?

_____

_____

_____

What are three things I have kept the same?

_____

_____

_____

What are three things I was reluctant to do, but did them anyway?

_____

_____

_____

What are three things I was reluctant to do, but want to next year?

_____

_____

_____

# Q & A Year Five 20 __ __

Name three likes –

_____
_____
_____

Name three dislikes –

_____
_____
_____

Name three good/easy things that happened this year –

_____
_____
_____

Name three bad/hard things that happened this year –

_____
_____
_____

What did I do for myself this year?

_____
_____
_____
_____

What did I do that did not support me this year?

_____
_____
_____
_____

# Q & A Year Five 20 __ __

If I could change one thing about myself, what would that be?

_____

_____

_____

If I could change one thing about my life, what would that be?

_____

_____

_____

If I could change one thing about the world, what would it be?

_____

_____

_____

What three things have I changed or done differently this year?

_____

_____

_____

What are three things I have kept the same?

_____

_____

_____

What are three things I was reluctant to do, but did them anyway?

_____

_____

_____

What are three things I was reluctant to do, but want to next year?

_____

_____

_____

## Create Your Own Topic _____

20___ ___ - _____

_____

_____

20___ ___ - _____

_____

_____

20___ ___ - _____

_____

_____

20___ ___ - _____

_____

_____

20___ ___ - _____

_____

_____

## Create Your Own Topic _____

20___ ___ - _____

_____

_____

20___ ___ - _____

_____

_____

20___ ___ - _____

_____

_____

20___ ___ - _____

_____

_____

20___ ___ - _____

_____

_____

# Year-End Summary

20__ __ - _____
_____
_____

20__ __ - _____
_____
_____

20__ __ - _____
_____
_____

20__ __ - _____
_____
_____

20__ __ - _____
_____
_____


# THE 5 YEAR JOURNAL Summary

_____
_____
_____
_____
_____
_____
_____
_____
_____
_____
_____
_____
_____

# About Doreene Clement

## by Sandy Rogers

**Doreene Clement** was a youngster when she began working in several Arizona restaurants that were owned and operated by her mother. Even at 11, she was naturally gifted as a people-person. It was here she learned about business and the value of self-reliance.

At 23 she purchased and completely revamped an already successful craft store in Greater Phoenix. Offering a welcome multi-faceted inventory of supplies and products, she developed extensive classes and workshops for the public.

One of Phoenix's primary television talk show hosts, Rita Davenport of "Open House with Rita Davenport", was already a daily staple for Metro Phoenix when they offered Doreene her own weekly craft demonstration segment.

Seeking for others to gain confidence in their own abilities, Doreene began producing a series of craft instruction books, which she designed, wrote and co-wrote. She also self-published and distributed them – attaining combined sales of over 1 million copies.

Next, the self-motivated and diversified entrepreneur created a highly successful residential and commercial painting company, based in Scottsdale, Arizona. Omni Painting was in business for over 20 years, successfully coloring Phoenix, The Valley of the Sun.

In 1999 Doreene self-published THE 5 YEAR JOURNAL, where the user can journal daily the next 5 years in just minutes a day. In 2002 she started her column, About Journaling, writing articles on how to keep a journal or diary.

In 2003 Doreene was diagnosed with two very rare types of breast cancer in both her breasts. She decided to manage her diagnosis using all natural methods and at one point in 2005 was declared to be cancer-free. As a cancer victor, which is the term she preferred over the more common term of cancer survivor, she wrote about her journey in a book that also included her personal journal entries. She titled the book *So Blessed: A Memoir – An Inspirational Exploration of Life and Living.* The definition of the word Blessed she used was Bless ed (bles'id) *adj.* **1.** Supported. **2.** Protected. **3.** Provided for. Doreene believed with her entire soul that she was indeed blessed.

The cancer journey left Doreene depleted not only physically but also financially. Emotionally and spiritually strong; however, Doreene was determined to be a cancer victor. Sadly, 4 years after her original diagnosis, Doreene made a conscious decision to release her physical body and made a peaceful transition at home on June 14, 2007. Sandy Rogers, was not only one of her best friends, she had also become her full time caregiver.

Before her transition, Doreene asked Sandy to make a promise to keep The 5 Year Journal available. She officially bequeathed and legally turned over all copyrights to The 5 Year Journal, all her articles, and all materials associated with The 5 Year Journal; as well as her unpublished book *So Blessed* that was fully edited and waiting for the right publisher to pick it up. Sandy, of course, promised to do her best to honor Doreene's wishes.

This new 2014 edition of The 5 Year Journal has been minimally edited, with primarily only the quotes on each page being changed, and will continue to provide the user with 5 years of insight and history.

Check the website at www.The5YearJournal.com for information or updates.

# About Sandy Rogers, CNP
## Certified Networker® Professional

 Sandy is best known as the 'Referral Queen' due to her reputation in the Greater Phoenix, Arizona Metropolitan area for connecting individuals and being a master referral resource to entrepreneurs in the holistic, spiritual, metaphysical and conscious business community. She is a strong proponent of supporting local business and is a charter member of Local First Arizona.

She has combined her 40 plus year of expertise in corporate sales, marketing and administration with creative entrepreneurial networking skills to build her list of connections and to assist others with their business needs.

Known for her engaging smile and warm heart, Sandy's vast experience encompasses event promotion and management, marketing, consulting, coaching and managing a variety of networking organizations.

In 2005 she received a certification from the Referral Institute® as a Certified Networker® Professional (CNP). Sandy's mission is to be the resource and connector for those who want to grow their small business through the power of referrals, building relationships and through word-of-mouth marketing.

The highest honor she has received was in caring for Doreene Clement for almost four years prior to her passing. When Doreene knew she was ready to leave her journey in this life she also knew she wanted The 5 Year Journal to live on. She entrusted Sandy with the publishing and copyrights to The 5 Year Journal. Doreene knew and had faith that Sandy would honor her work and would help to keep the legacy of The 5 Year Journal alive.

You can learn more about Sandy and her work at www.AskSandyRogers.com

CPSIA information can be obtained
at www.ICGtesting.com
Printed in the USA
BVHW052253141121
621494BV00006B/350